THE

TRUTH ABOUT

INVESTING

BACK TO BASICS

SEAN COOPER, CFA

THE TRUTH ABOUT INVESTING
BACK TO BASICS

ISBN-13: 978-1534667297

ISBN-10: 1534667296

Table of Contents

Acknowledgements

First, to my younger sister Kendra Kessler, for her time and diligence in editing my original manuscript. Without your patience and care, my finance oriented mind would have left readers with an even dryer experience, replete with grammatical errors. Thank you for being gentle with my ego in the editing process. Not every editor would have been so kind.

To my fiancée, Anastasia Peterson, my parents, Merrell and Margo Cooper, my younger brother, Danny Cooper, and brother in-law, Kyle Kessler. Thank you for your continued support throughout the writing process and all of your encouragement to not give up on the publishing process. I love you all.

To my cousin, Shane Spears, for providing the excellent articles on psychology that fueled an entire chapter of this book. Thank you for your support and insights.

To, Mike Waldo, my high school teacher, friend, and mentor, thank you for pushing me down the path of business. Without your guidance I would never have found my true calling in finance. Your lessons, mentorship, and support have been invaluable.

To Josh and Ciri Sayler, for believing in me and believing that this project would, one day, come to fruition. Your friendship means the world to me.

To Marco Cummings, Darrell Stern, and Jesse Bernal, thank you for aiding in the production of the copy on the back cover. Jesse, thank you for the introduction to Alex Changho. Alex, thank you for being the catalyst to bring this project full circle and seeing it through to publication.

To the many people I have not named specifically here but who provided their support and guidance along the way, of which there were many, Thank You!

About the Author

     Sean Cooper was born in Des Moines, Iowa to Merrell and Margo Cooper on May, 29th 1987. He grew up in Morton, Washington where he attended 1st through 12th grade, playing as much soccer as possible along the way. After graduating from high school he moved to Denver, Colorado to attend the University of Denver where he received his BSBA with a major in finance just two and a half years later.

     The first couple of years of Sean's finance career started only three days after graduation when he began work as a Market

Research Intern and Internal Wholesaler at Jackson National Life. While at Jackson, Sean attained his Colorado Life and Health Insurance license, as well as the Series 6, 63, 7, and 66 licenses. He later moved to one of Jackson's subsidiaries, National Planning Corporation, where he worked three and a half years as a Business Development Consulting. As a BDC, Sean, worked with financial advisors to educate them on the WEALTHONE platform, aid them in the conversion to a fee-based practice, and familiarized them with the various third party asset managers available. While working for NPC he also attained his MBA with a finance focus from the University of Colorado: Denver.

In 2014 Sean starting his own Registered Investment Advisory firm, Fit Financial Consulting LLC, where he works with individuals and families on budgeting, portfolio construction and management, and financial plans. His primary goal is to provide families with financial education to improve their financial fitness, much the same way you would seek to improve your physical fitness. In a continued effort to improve his own financial knowledge base, Sean enrolled in the CFA® Program to obtain the highest set of credentials in the global investment management industry and now holds both the Chartered Financial Analyst® and Certified Financial Planner® designations.

When he is not working with clients or studying, Sean enjoys working out at CrossFit Banshee, playing soccer, hiking, relaxing at a family cabin in the mountains, hanging out with family and friends, or going to the movies.

Sean holds the Chartered Financial Analyst® designation and lives in Washington State.

In the Beginning

Why Did People Invest?

Why do you invest? You invest to make money, right? But how do you invest to make money? For most people, this involves buying a stock or a mutual fund and selling it at a higher price. People buy mutual funds and exchange traded funds (ETFs) with the expectation that in a few years, months, weeks, or, most cases, even days, it will appreciate in value. Chances are you know a few or if you are lucky, all, of the mutual funds, etc., that you are invested in. However, there is a very strong chance you cannot form a strong logical reason for why you are invested in those particular funds, except that your financial advisor told you they would provide strong diversification.

Do you know what those funds invest in, what their investment objective is, or how they fit into your portfolio? Most people do not. Most people can tell you which of their funds have performed exceptionally well, but that is about it. This is not enough. People have lost sight of what an investment really is and what they are really getting into. So too, have investors' expectations been completely distorted.

People originally invested for the same reason as we do today, but with much different expectations and a much greater understanding of the agreement they were entering. Do not get me wrong, people have always, and will always invest to make money. However, people have not always invested blindly.

This shift is due to a multitude of factors. Accessibility, specialization, and responsibility are the three primary changes that have re-sculpted the investing landscape. I will touch more on accessibility in the chapter on the evolution of investing. For now, let's focus on specialization and responsibility.

When I refer to specialization, I am not talking about anything new to any first world country. In fact, we have witnessed specialization in nearly every field imaginable for centuries. Personally, I am glad that is the case. Let's say, for example, you have a clot in your brain. The bad news is, this clot could prove life threatening if not operated on as soon as possible. The good news is, it is operable and there is a very high likelihood of success. I for one would be very grateful to that general/family practice doctor who identified the abnormality. Although his training included a vast amount of information on the functionality of the brain, surgery, and how to operate on the brain, I would be even more grateful to that doctor for referring me to a specialist. Specifically, a brain surgeon who spends every hour of his working day, operating on brains and dealing with patients going into brain surgery. The fact that the brain surgeon has specialized, means he has made his profession an art form. His experience will lead to fewer errors, lower likelihood of complications, and knowhow of what to do should certain complications arise.

The same holds true for any profession. Lawyers have completely different bar exams for different areas of law. Henry Ford saw the value of specialization in automotive production in the early 1900s. Rather than having a single worker, (or group of workers), build a car from start to finish, he had each worker focus on a single task in the overall production of every vehicle. In this way, each worker become an expert at the task they were assigned. They made fewer errors and were much faster in their work.

Hence the natural evolution of investing, which I will discuss in more detail in the next chapter. Suffice it to say, that instead of each individual taking time out of their busy schedules to determine what they were going to invest in and when they were going to invest, they began to rely on specialists. These specialists appeared at multiple levels and in multiple roles. From the everyday investor's point of view, there are mutual fund managers and financial advisors who both specialize in investing to different degrees. While the financial advisor specializes in financial planning (aiding individuals and families in planning for retirement, saving for college, as well as many major financial decisions), the mutual fund manager specializes in managing the actual investment. Essentially, the financial advisor is doing research to choose the "best" mutual funds for your portfolio and the mutual fund manager is choosing the "best" securities to hold within that mutual fund.

Interestingly, that is just the beginning of the specialization. Not only are their specialized mutual funds for every sector, country, style, objective, and market capitalization that you can wish to invest in, there are a multitude of analysts that support each mutual fund manager with very specific research mandates.

The increasing degrees of specialization have served two purposes. The intended purpose was to improve investment outcomes and save people time. The unintended consequence was a growing gap between investors and their investments.

This brings me back to my original point. Why did people invest? People use to invest for ownership in a company.

Ownership

Ownership is the foundation of investing. Sure, people own a car or two and probably even a home. Very few people, though, have the fortitude to own a company, let alone someone else's company. Yet this is what hundreds of millions of people do on a daily basis by purchasing shares in a mutual fund without even realizing it. Even the savvy investor who understands conceptually that they are purchasing a percentage of a company by buying its shares, rarely thinks of themselves as an owner of a company. Yet that is exactly what you are.

Early investors understood this explicitly. This firm grasp of reality stemmed from the position those investors were in at the time they invested. Most investors in the early stages of the financial markets had already taken care of all of life's necessities (food, clothing, shelter, etc.) as well as most of life's wants (entertainment, better modes of transportation, leisure, vacation, etc.) and wanted to use their savings to further bolster their lot in life. The question became how to make your money work for you. It is a really rough problem to have too; you are already successful, you want to make more money, but you do not want to use more of your time to do so. So you invest.

The solution seems obvious today, but was a long time in the making. Early investing meant giving, and trusting, another entrepreneur with your hard earned money. Joe Blow decides he is going to open a restaurant but he does not have enough money to purchase the building site where he wants to open. This is where investing comes into play. In most cases, people had to pay cash for a home, land, equipment, and virtually everything they needed for daily life and to run a business. A loan, was a revolutionary idea that allowed people to purchase something now and pay it off over time, plus accrued interest of course. This is where the idea of an investment came from. The challenge for the average person to offer a loan was the very same reason loans came into existence. The average person did not have enough capital to fork out to own something outright. Hence the development of banks.

Banks offered a safe haven for your excess cash; a place where it was more difficult for robbers to steal money. Over time, bank owners saw the need for loans and came up with the idea of lending this pooled money to people based on the promise that those people would repay the principle borrowed with interest. Subsequently, banks also set up savings accounts in which people could let their money sit while earning a small interest rate. The difference between the amount paid to individuals in their savings accounts and the amount paid to the bank by borrowers was the banks' profit.

The same concept applied to wealthy investors. Although most people could not afford to lend money on an individual basis, many wealthy people had the excess funds on hand to make individual loans. Two subgroups eventually broke out between these wealthy individuals. One was the infamous loan shark. When an individual needed money but did not have a strong enough credit rating to get a loan from the bank, they could go to a loan shark to get the money they needed. Unfortunately, loan sharks demanded a higher interest rate for the loans they made and often enforced their "contracts" in less than traditional manners.

A more socially acceptable source of individual funding was that of the venture capitalist. These individuals not only made loans to entrepreneurs but would often seek out potential business opportunities in which they could invest as a partner by supplying only capital without taking part in the day to day practices of the business. For the entrepreneur, this meant either repaying the initial investment of the venture capitalist with interest or sharing in the profit of the business in return for the capital the investor provided and the risk they took on in doing so.

This results in two methods of making money in return for providing the capital needed to start, fund, and keep the operations of a business running. The first method would be to sell your share/ownership/stake in the company for more than you originally paid for that stake. In today's terms, that is simply a matter of the stock positions held going up in value. This could occur for a multitude of reason. Perhaps the manager of a large mutual fund was in a good mood on a particular day and took a large stake in the company you held shares of. Maybe the general market trend has been up and your stock has just been riding the wave. Or, better yet, the company actually announced revenue and earnings above and beyond what was expected by analysts spurring a wave of investments. Any of these, seemingly unrelated, and often irrelevant events, could affect the price of your shares.

In the early stages of investing however, this was not the case. Even a wealthy investor could probably only provide capital to one or two ventures at a time. If you were going to invest your hard earned money in a business, often with an individual you previously did not know, you would be damn sure you thought that venture was going to succeed. That meant doing your homework. You would want to see a thorough business plan, analyze all of the estimates and forecasts the business owner had made regarding demand, sales, cost, and profits, and feel good about not only the business itself but the individual that was going to be running it.

Provided you were going to take so much time to evaluate your investment, you were probably going to be in it for the long haul too. You would not suffer unease about your investment because of the whims of a friend or coworker. The election of a new president would have little to no effect on the business venture, you knew this, and were not going to make your investment decisions on it. There were hundreds or even thousands of local and outside events that were completely irrelevant to your investment. You were a rational decision maker and you were going to sit on your investment for as long as it had potential. In fact, it could take several years for your venture to turn a profit. And 10 or more years to be well enough established to draw the attention of larger investors with enough capital to take over the business or assist in the expansion of the business. The time was of little consequence though given the time and energy you had invested in your research, you were reasonably sure of a large payout in the end.

The first method of making money through an investment was to sell your stake for more than you originally purchased it for, or invested into the venture. As a partial owner of the business that sale involved other individuals or businesses going through the very same process you went through in your original assessment of the venture. These new investors wanted to be sure their investment was a sound one, that the new business would fit in well with the current business model, and that they could reasonably expect the new acquisition to continue to grow and prosper. Simply put, this is the daily dealings in mergers, acquisitions, and corporate takeovers.

Dividends

In the absence of a larger entity buying out your stake in your new venture, you could still count on a stream of income in return for your investment. A commonly overlooked investment strategy today is that of a dividend focus. Years ago, this was the primary, if not the only means of seeing a return on your investment. Due to the degree of risk you assumed in fronting the money for a new venture, you were entitled to share in the profits of that new venture.

As I previously mentioned, turning a profit could easily take several years. But if you had invested wisely, the payoff was great. Say, for example, a man walked up to you who wanted to open up a new grocery store (the first and only grocery store) in your small town. Now, this man had the knowhow, the idea, the drive, the time and everything else he needed to start and operate a successful grocery store. The one thing he was lacking was the capital. So the two of you strike up a deal. Since you have some excess funds just lying around, you are going to provide all of the investment capital for the grocery store and the man is going to provide all of the human capital. In return for your investment, the two of you are going to split the profits the store generates 50/50.

Provided the store does generate a profit, this could be a very substantial payout. As you can see, this is quite different from investing for dividends today. While some stronger dividend paying companies might achieve a 3-5% payout on a regular basis, very few are above that. Also, that 3-5% is as a percentage of your investment, not of profits. You certainly are not going to come even close to the payout ratio of 50%, unless of course you actually own 50% of the company. Despite this difference, the concept is still very much the same. In return for lending a company your money and taking on the risk of losing that money, the company is agreeing to share in any profits it is not going to re-invest in for growth or supply purposes.

Again, venture capitalists invested a substantial part of their life savings into these new businesses. For that reason, they were willing to wait quite some time to reap their rewards. Jumping from one venture to another meant missing out on the profitable periods of an investment. In turn, this led to far greater stability within the investment market. People were not chasing profits. Instead they realized part of the equation to earning a return was not just the investment itself but time. Even today, with record swings and choppy markets, consistent dividend paying stocks, and preferred stock in particular have weathered the market swing far better than the equity market as a whole.

Research

I mentioned before, the vast amount of time a venture capitalist would invest in researching their potential businesses. Now let's take a closer look at what that really entails. Much like a bank manager does today when evaluating whether or not they are going to grant a loan to an entrepreneur, a venture capitalist wants to see a business plan and will read it in its entirety. A strong business plan will include the business concept, the product or service, the market, the marketing strategy, the production plans, personnel, and financial plans. Have you ever read an annual report? No? Most people have not. A company's annual report is very similar to a business plan though, containing much of the same information.

Although capital was often garnered from friends and family, oftentimes entrepreneurs would have to go to an unknown source for the funding they required. In this scenario, the venture capitalist would also need to take time to get to know the entrepreneur. Over the course of many meetings, lunches, dinners, other social events, talking with the entrepreneur's references, friends and family, the venture capitalist would get to know his newfound business partner intimately. You would not hand a large sum of money to a complete stranger and trust them to return it to you, and neither would the savvy venture capitalist. Have you ever met the CEO of one of the companies you invested in, or the head fund manager of one of your mutual funds? No? Me neither. And I probably will not meet the vast majority of them. But that does not prevent me or you from getting to know them to the best of our abilities.

The venture capitalist would also perform their own analysis of the feasibility of success for the proposed venture. Rather than simply trusting the entrepreneurs researching and taking their word for it, the wise investor would seek to confirm, or deny, the entrepreneurs findings. Will demand really support a grocery store in our town? Will we be able to get supplies at a reasonable cost from the next nearest community? Does the entrepreneur have the capacity to manage the store, keep items stocked, and handle the financial reporting of the company?

Furthermore, the venture capitalist will evaluate their own resolve; asking themselves dozens of questions. Can I afford to leave this money untouched for at least 10 years? Can I stomach potentially losing my entire investment? What alternative investments can I find? Would I be happier doing something else with my money? Am I going to change my mind in the next few months or even the next few years? Have you ever asked yourself these questions? If not, you are doing yourself, and the company you are investing in, a huge disservice.

Evolution of Investing

Venture Capitalist

I have already spoken in detail about the venture capitalist. You can see how much time and effort an investor of their caliber put into determining the appropriate business in which to invest. It is not surprising either, considering any one venture may be the only business they invest in for the next 10 years or more. There is no room for error when you have all of your money in one place. That is why the Venture Capitalist spent so much time doing research on their potential investments. They wanted to ensure all of the odds were stacked in their favor to ensure the success of the company with which they were investing. Even a slight miscalculation could spell disaster for these early adaptors of the investment world.

Aside from the vast amount of research put into each and every investment, the venture capitalist had an additional method for mitigating their risk. The method is really very simple, but may seem foreign in comparison to investment strategies today. Buy and hold is nothing new to the investment world. Today's investors may even sneer at such a simplistic investment approach. Some may even say that buy and hold has gone the way of the dinosaurs.

However, there is one great advantage to a buy and hold strategy that is commonly overlooked. It is not that most investors are not aware of this advantage. Instead, it is the general shortsightedness of the investment industry that has led to the dismissal of the buy and hold approach.

Simply put, holding onto the same investment over an extended period of time tends to reduce the volatility of expected returns over that period of time. For an easily understandable example, lets take a look at the S&P 500 from 1928-2000. The average one year return of the S&P 500 for this period was 12.66%. Unfortunately, the standard deviation is also incredibly high at 20.25%.

As you can see, an investor could have made substantial gains in any particular year. The greatest gain was made in 1933 to the tune of 54.00%. Unfortunately, the very same investor could have experienced substantial losses nearly as often as gains had their holding period only been this single year. The greatest loss for the S&P 500 was in 1931 with a return of -43.40%. What is more, picking those years in which the S&P 500 was up, as opposed to down is nearly impossible.

If we extend our holding period to 10 years, the story is altogether different. Over a 10 year period the absolute worst you could have done was an annual loss of -0.89% from 1929-1938. That is considerably less than the one year loss of -43.40% mentioned above. On the other hand, the greatest gain you could have expected from any 10 year period between 1928 and 2000 was from 1949-1958. This is a far cry from the one year return posted by the S&P in 1933. I think most people would be quite content with an average return of 11.36%, though given such a significant reduction in volatility. Specifically, reducing your worst case scenario from -43.40% over a one year period to -0.89% over a ten year period. I think most people would happily take 1.30% (12.66% down to 11.36%) less in annual returns to reduce their risk by 14.67% (20.25% down to 5.58%).

This is not to say that you will not experience one year losses in excess of -43.40%. It does suggest that if you hold strong to your investment,(do not allow that one year loss to affect your investment decisions and subsequently sell your holdings), over a ten year time frame your expected average return will be much smoother than buying and selling on a regular basis.

The real problem stems from the investor themselves. Far too frequently an investor will witness a loss in their portfolio and lose their nerve right at the last second. At the crucial moment, they make the decision to liquidate their holdings, potentially even moving to cash, only to sit idly by and watch their holdings recover without them because they got out at the very bottom. The benefits of a long term investment strategy are completely negated by frequent buying and selling.

Buying and selling at the wrong time is the very reason the average equity investor's performance so grossly underperformed the S&P 500. According to the 2012 Dalbar Study, in 2011 the average asset allocation investor experienced a return of -1.27% while the S&P 500 was up 2.12%. Below is a table showing additional rates of return for the average investor as compared to the S&P 500, the Barclays Aggregate Bond Index, and inflation.

Annualized Return	Average Asset Allocation Investor	S&P 500	Barclays Aggregate Bond Index	Inflation
20 Years	2.12%	7.81%	6.50%	2.56%
10 Years	1.11%	2.92%	5.78%	2.62%
5 Years	-1.48%	-0.25%	6.50%	2.54%
3 Years	7.57%	14.11%	6.77%	2.38%
1 Year	-1.27%	2.12%	7.84%	2.96%

(Dalbar 2012)

The graph below takes another look at the Dalbar Study over a different period and in a slightly different way. The result is the same.

Investor Returns: not the same as *Investment* Returns

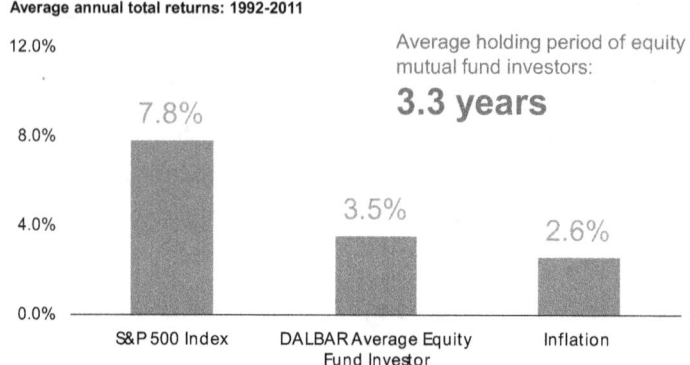

Average annual total returns: 1992-2011

Average holding period of equity mutual fund investors:

3.3 years

S&P 500 Index — 7.8%
DALBAR Average Equity Fund Investor — 3.5%
Inflation — 2.6%

Source: "Quantitative Analysis of Investor Behavior, 2012," DALBAR, Inc.; used with permission. For illustrative purposes only. Past performance does not guarantee future results. The S&P 500 is an unmanaged, weighted index comprising 500 widely held common stocks varying in composition and is unavailable for direct investment. Average Equity Fund Investor is comprised of the cash flow of 4,585 equity funds as classified by ICI (Investment Company Institute). The returns are represented by the change in total equity mutual fund assets after excluding sales, redemptions and exchanges. This method of calculation captures realized and unrealized capital gains, dividends, interest, trading costs, sales charges, fees, expenses and any other costs. After calculating investor returns in dollar terms, two percentages are calculated for the period examined. Performance calculated assumes reinvestment of all dividends and capital gains. Total return rate is determined by calculating the investor return dollars as a percentage of the net of the sales, redemptions, and exchanges for the period. Holding period reflects the length of time the average investor holds a fund if the current redemption rate persists. It is the time required to fully redeem the account. Retention rates are expressed in years and fractions of years. Over the time period 1992-2011, the average equity fund investor held their mutual funds for an average of 3.3 years.

 UBS

Not for public use. Not to be quoted, shown or mailed to clients.

6

(UBS 2012)

Individual Stocks/Shareholder

Finding an individual who was willing to invest such a substantial sum in your enterprise was very difficult though. The solution to this dilemma was surprisingly simple. In using the assets of a venture capitalist a business owner often gave up partial ownership of their company. From that point it was not much of a stretch to imagine splitting a company, or at least its ownership, into even smaller portions. Hence the idea of a share, literally a share of a company. And so, stock was born.

Okay, maybe it was not quite that fast. The progression from the idea of partial shares of a company to stock certificates was not altogether too difficult though. First, you had a select few investors with large sums to invest that could fund a small startup by themselves. Second, you expand the idea of partial ownership to split the company into smaller pieces, and make it easier for the average person to invest. This was mutually beneficial for the investor as well as the entrepreneur. Investors could diversify their risk by investing in multiple companies since the initial investment required by each individual was small. It was also easier for the entrepreneur to find potential investors due to the reduced investment requirements. Third, the investors wanted some sort of proof of their ownership and entitlement to future profits. Originally, some sort of legal documentation and signatures were required to be created by the parties involved. Over time though, a standard document was developed to serve this purpose. This evolved into a stock certificate. So too did the phrase shareholder come to be, to represent those who owned a share in a company or held stock certificates.

Today virtually everything is done electronically. Many people have never even heard of a stock certificate, much less seen one. Typically a custodian acts as a middle man to hold the funds and certificates of shareholders. This is designed to prevent errors in reporting, the appropriation of funds, lost or stolen documents, and aids in dispute resolution between parties.

Mutual Funds

The next step in the evolution of investing was in the form of management. Most people wanted to invest. Who does not want to let their money sit and make more money for them without having to lift a finger? This is exactly the problem. People wanted to invest but they did not want to invest the time and energy necessary to determine what was a good investment. Entrepreneurs saw the need and made themselves experts on the financial markets.

These "experts" on the financial markets came in two forms. One was the person to person, financial advisor. These people offered to do the research on various stocks and provide advice to you on which stocks to invest in, in exchange for a fee. The second person was the manager who, rather than dealing directly with individuals, let the financial advisors direct individuals to their funds. That is right; they did their own research to blend individual securities together into pre-built portfolios. Of course, the initial research was only the first step, these newly proclaimed mutual fund managers also provided ongoing research and oversight of their funds to ensure all of the investments still met their investment standards.

Everyday investors now had multiple means of investing without necessarily being knowledgeable about investing. You could hire an individual to help you build a personalized portfolio to meet your individual goals and needs, often utilizing mutual funds and individual securities, or you could rely on a group of mutual fund managers to choose the best investments for you based on their individual mandates. This meant you could do a minimal amount of research to choose a few mutual funds that fit your needs and let the managers do the rest.

Aside from the relatively minimal upfront legwork on your part in choosing a mutual fund, there were two other key benefits that made these investments popular. First, the mutual fund manager was there to continually monitor the investment. They were supposed to be watching out for stocks that would make better investments than those currently held and also get rid of the ones that were no longer profitable. More importantly, mutual funds offered additional diversification. By pooling many investors' funds, hundreds or even thousands of securities could be purchased at once. Investors who were once only able to choose a single business to invest in could now buy shares in a single mutual fund and immediately own thousands of companies at once. As we all know, since it has been drilled into us since the early 20th century, diversification reduces risk. It is common sense that by owning several businesses, the chances of losing all of your money due to those businesses going bankrupt is greatly reduced.

It is surprising however that mutual funds did not become a popular investment vehicle until the late 1970's and early 1980's. Both actively managed and passively managed mutual funds are still popular today. Although mutual funds are the most popular form of investment today, another means of investing is rapidly growing in popularity.

ETFs and Fund of Funds

ETFs (exchange traded funds) and fund of funds are a natural evolution of the financial market.

First let's discuss fund of funds. The primary reason for the development of a financial vehicle like a fund of funds is the very same reason for the development of mutual funds. By offering a fund of funds, an investor now only had to choose a single fund of funds as opposed to choosing several mutual funds. This further reduced the time spent in the research process and offered even greater diversification, all in one fell swoop.

ETFs on the other hand are an evolution of index funds. First of all, index funds are a specific type of mutual fund. Many research firms like Standard & Poors and Russell, have indexes that are used to track different sectors of the market. For example, you have probably heard of the S&P 500 which tracks 500 US stocks based on market size, liquidity, and industry grouping. You may have even heard of the Russell 2000 or the MSCI EAFE which track the performance of the 2,000 smallest companies in the Russell 3000 Index (the 3,000 biggest U.S. stocks) and indexes from Europe, Australia, and Southeast Asia, respectively. Unfortunately, you cannot invest in these indexes directly. Instead, mutual fund managers created funds that track these indexes which you can invest in, hence the index fund. The primary drawback to an index fund, though, is the cost. The highest cost a mutual fund has is that of paying for the mutual fund manager. This cost, among others, directly detracts from the investor's performance. For that reason, investors strove to create alternate, more cost efficient means of investing in these indexes.

ETFs fit that bill perfectly. An ETF typically does not have a manager, *per se,* and, therefore, has much lower cost. It does, however, strive to track one of many indexes as closely as possible. Due to the fact that ETFs track an index of some sort, trading costs are also kept to a minimum. In fact, most ETFs only reconstitute once a year, reallocating funds to more closely represent the index it represents.

Of course this brings up the debate between active and passive management. Essentially, the argument stems from market efficiency and market inefficiency. Active money managers argue that the market is inefficient and, therefore, an investor can take advantage of mispricing and price swings in the market in order to increase their returns. Pacifists argue that the market is efficient and the best you can do is to simply ride the wave, while being adequately diversified, of course. A less aggressive form of the pacifist belief is not necessarily complete market efficiency but that the mispricing is so minute, happens so fast, or the cost of taking advantage of that mispricing is such that you will not actually benefit by doing so. Whatever you believe, you have probably used one of these forms of investments, if not several of them. In the end, the result is much the same.

Detachment

Through the vast transitions the financial markets have taken, people have become more and more removed from the individual
18

investments. Layer upon layer has been added to increase the ease of investing, the ease of diversifying, and to reduce the amount of research individuals need to complete in order to invest. The Warren Buffett style investor is a dying breed.

We have all heard of Warren Buffet. We all know he is an extremely successful investor and business man. But why? What makes Mr. Buffett so successful? According to Nikki Ross in the book Lessons from the Legends of Wall Street,

> "Buffett thinks of buying stocks as if he were buying a piece of business to hold for the long term. He looks for companies that have a track record of financial success, quality management, a wide competitive advantage, and superior brand-name products used repeatedly. Generally, he purchases firms generating dependable streams of earnings that can be reinvested to grow the business and produce high returns on money invested by shareholders. Before buying a stock, Buffett asks: 'Is this a wonderful business? Is the stock selling at a reasonable price?'"
>
> "Although Buffett buys stocks he plans to hold for at least ten years and his favorite holding period coincides with his favorite life expectancy—forever—this does not mean he never sells sooner…After Buffett buys stocks, he continues to monitor his holdings against his buying criteria. Regardless of earnings setbacks, Buffett will hold a stock he has bought for the long term if he believes the firm will continue to have good earnings growth in the future. And he may use wide market fluctuations in the stock or the general market as opportunities to buy more shares."
> (Ross 2000)

Sadly, the age of Buffett is coming to an end. That does not mean that it should or that it has to, however! In fact, a wave of Buffett style investing could very well be the greatest thing to ever happen to the financial markets. Now, I am not necessarily talking about value investing or taking quite as much time as Buffett does in analyzing a potential investment opportunity. I am, however, advocating getting to know your investments and potential investments far more intimately than the average investor today does and holding those investments for the long term.

Think about it: if everyone took more time to understand their investments, to gain a firm grasp on what they could reasonably expect from their investments, and held those investments for the long term, where would the volatility come from? If every investor knew their individual holdings so well that they were comfortable holding those investments for at least 10 years and actually followed through on their strategy of holding for at least 10 years, as Buffett does, volatility in the markets would be dramatically reduced. Ironically, with reduced volatility, people would be more comfortable holding their investments for long periods of time. And so the cycle goes...

Investing Today: 1990's Can Do No Wrong

Unfortunately for today's investors, volatility is very much alive and well. Furthermore, expectations are dramatically out of whack. This is due largely to the short time frames most people have in terms of investment experience. A large portion of investors today began investing in the 1980's and 1990's. With the exception of 1987, this period was composed entirely of bull markets. The concept of a monkey throwing a dart at the financial pages of the Wall Street Journal to choose investments was not too far off. With a few exceptions, it did not matter what you invested in, you were going to make money.

Anyone investing in equity was virtually guaranteed a strong return. The same held true for bonds too. As interest rates have trended downward for the last 30 years, the value of a bond portfolio has actually gone up.

As a financial advisor or a mutual fund manager, you could do no wrong. All you had to do was follow the trends and ride the wave. Clients were happy with their investments. Everyone thought themselves an investment genius.

This is how we began the 21st century. Expectations of returns were at all-time highs and the need for sound investment advice and detailed research was at an all-time low. Eventually gravity sets in though. It should come as no surprise that the old mantra of, heeding the lessons of history or risk history repeating itself, would become a reality. Anyone who read about the tulip fiasco in Western Europe from 1634-1638, or the South Sea frenzy in 1720 and witnessed what was going on with tech stocks would have gotten out. And indeed they would have, if it was not for the mob mentality of the markets. No one wanted to miss out on the massive profits being made in technology so people increased their allocation instead of taking their profits. This was the case until investment funds could no-longer support the ultra-high prices of tech stocks and the subsequent crash of 2000-2002 ensued, further aggravated by the attacks of 9/11.

2000's Expect Everything to Be Gold (12%)

The beginning of the 21st century marked a drastic shift in expectations and true chaos. Early on, people still demanded the 12% average return of the S&P 500 that they had experienced for the last two decades. Fund managers and financial advisors alike were under fire. They strove to find new investments that would bring the returns their clients demanded but nothing existed that could support these return expectations for any length of time. The memory of 2000-2002 did not even seem to help. Investors soon forgot the dramatic losses they had withstood, or remembered all too well their losses and shot for the moon as they tried desperately to repair their retirement nest egg. In either case, expectations were not in alignment with what the market had to offer.

By 2007, the markets were running rampant once more with bullish claims and unreasonable investment expectations. 2008 brought an end to all that. Trading between equity and fixed income securities or even cash became the new norm as investors sought safety. Even now, more than three years after the end of the great recession, vast sums still sit on the side lines in cash. Financial advisors and fund managers are again at a disadvantage and unable to keep their clients happy.

Goals have changed though. Investors want first and foremost to protect their assets. After two dramatic pullbacks in the market in a single decade, people are not willing to risk a third. Expectations, however, have not realigned. Yes, people want protection from another pullback, but so too, do they want to participate in the bull runs to rebuild their portfolios. Much like the age of Warren Buffett, the concept of strategic investing and diversification, are dying. It does not mean they should, though. I will talk more about this and the idea of active, tactical management, in later sections.

Do Not Lose Money

Emotion Driven Market

Volatility seems to be the worst enemy of the financial markets. The greater the volatility in the market, the more people watch their portfolios. The more people watch their portfolios the more susceptible they become to making irrational buying and selling decisions. The more irrational decisions that are made, the more volatile the market becomes. And so the cycle goes.

The following is a graph of the volatility index plotted against the State Street Consumer Confidence Index. The volatility index, or VIX, is a measure of the overall volatility of the financial markets. Essentially the VIX looks at the price patterns of the market and measures how much it changes on a daily basis. The wider the price range, or the more frequent the swing of the market, the higher the VIX will go. The narrower the price range, or the less frequent the price swings, the lower the VIX will go. The State Street Investor Confidence Index, or ICI, is a measure of the general populations overall outlook on the market. When the ICI is up, it suggests that most people have a positive outlook on the market. When the majority of investors are bearish on the market, the ICI is down.

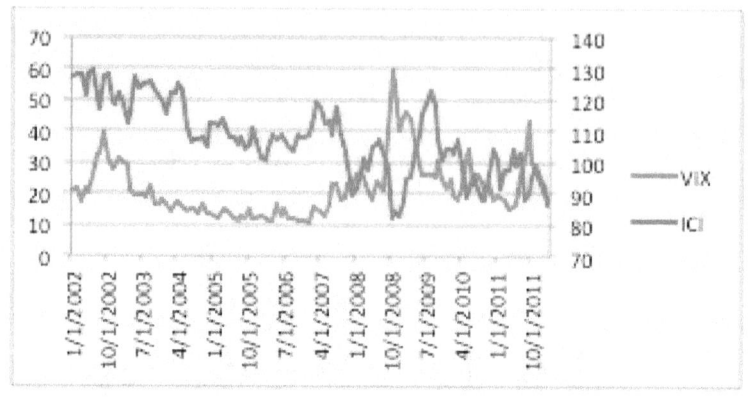

(CBOE 2012)(State Street Global Markets 2012)

As you can see from this chart, the VIX and the ICI tend to react opposite to one another. While this might not be immediately apparent from the chart, the numbers make the point far more poignant.

Correlation is a measure of how closely two series of numbers move together and ranges from negative one to positive one. A correlation score of negative one means the number sets react completely opposite to one another. Therefore, when one set is down, the other set is up directly in proportion to the reduction in the first set. For example, if one set of data goes from 10, up to 20, down to 5. A set with a perfect negative correlation could go from 20, down to 0, up to 30.

A correlation score of positive one means just the opposite. Sets of numbers with a perfect positive correlation of one will react exactly in sync with one another. Therefore, when one set is down, the other set will also be down directly in proportion to the first set. Using the same example as above, if one set of data goes from 10, up to 20, down to 5. A second set with a correlation of positive one could go from 20, up to 40, down to 10.

Correlations between these two extremes can also occur. Any negative correlation means the data sets tend to act opposite to one another, but not necessarily all of the time and not always proportionately. The same holds true for any positive correlation. In which case, the data sets will tend to act in conjunction to one another, but not all of the time and not always proportionally. A correlation of zero is a different story all together. Zero actually means that there is no correlation between the data sets and you have no capability of predicting how one set of data will react based on what the other data sets do.

With that said, the correlation between the VIX and the ICI from January 2002, through February of 2012 was -.3211. I think this makes it a little clearer than the graph by itself that the VIX and the ICI tend to act opposite to one another. Meaning, as consumer confidence decreases, volatility increases. In contrast, as consumer confidence increases, volatility decreases.

The fact that the VIX and ICI react opposite to one another lends credence to the concept that we are our own worst enemies. The less confidence we have in the market, the more we trade irrationally, creating volatility. The more volatility, the less confident we are in the market, the more irrational investment decisions we make.

It is a vicious cycle at that. It is the cycle we have been in since the beginning of 2008 and was showing signs of rearing its ugly head as early as 1999. It is a cycle that has no easy resolution. But there is a way out. This brings me to the truth about investing. I mentioned earlier that volatility seems to be the worst enemy of the financial markets. The truth, though, is that volatility would have no detrimental effect in the absence of emotion. Investor emotion is the bane of investing.

If you were never worried or concerned over your investment losing money, why would you sell your holdings? The only reason you would exit your positions is if you needed the money. Earnings, cash flow, world news, terrorist attacks, presidential elections, none of these things would affect your investment decision. Maybe they should not. If you think about it, if emotion was removed from the market, and no-one sold their shares unless they needed the money, (as long as there were more people contributing to their investments as opposed to taking money out to pay for expenses), the financial market would only trend up; a nice...steady...bull market.

Obviously this is not a realistic goal. It can be achieved to a certain extent, though, if we analyze what drives investor emotion. One primary cause would be volatility. This is a secondary and not a leading cause, however. Similarly, the recent market trends, which have driven continued volatility, are a secondary cause of increased investor emotion. So what spurs investor's original emotional responses and subsequent irrational decision? We will examine these causes over the next couple of chapters. First, let's look at how managers are striving to accommodate the current demands of clients.

Timing the Markets

As expectations continue to exceed market realities, fund managers and financial advisors are continuously looking for new methods to make their clients' money and/or prevent losing their money. For years a strategic approach to investing was preached from every corner of the financial globe. The idea behind a strategic investment is to buy and hold a grouping of securities over an extended period of time.

Step one, determine your risk tolerance to determine the overall allocation of your portfolio. A very aggressive portfolio might be invested 100% in equities; where as a moderate portfolio might be 50% equities and 50% bonds. Of course this is a very broad view of the portfolio. Although a simple 50%/50% portfolio meets the criteria of a strategic portfolio, it fails to take into account what is actually held within those two opposing investments.

The equity portion might consist of domestic, international, and emerging stocks ranging from small cap to large cap and from value to growth. The bond portion could consist of government bonds such as U.S. treasuries anywhere from 1 month to 20+ years as well as corporate debt ranging from very high quality AAA ratings to junk bonds with ratings BB and below. Other asset classes may include commodities, TIPS (treasury inflation protected securities), real estate, and currencies. The point is, from your original risk assessment, you can get a general idea of the appropriate allocation of your portfolio and from there you can greatly diversify your portfolio with various asset classes that are non-correlated. Therefore step two is to diversify your portfolio with non-correlated assets.

Step one provides you with an asset allocation designed to provide the optimal return given your risk tolerance. What do I mean by risk tolerance? Let's take a simple example. We will assume you only have two investment options, the S&P 500 (IVV) to represent the equity side of your investment and the Barclay Capital Aggregate Bond Fund (AGG) to represent the bond side of your investment. Below is a chart that shows the return of various, blended portfolios consisting of these two investments for 2008 and 2009. (This performance includes dividend payments but not necessarily the reinvestment thereof).

	Equity/Bond					
Year	100%/0%	80%/20%	60%/40%	40%/60%	20%/80%	0%/100%
2008	-33.40%	-25.68%	-17.96%	-10.25%	-2.53%	5.19%
2009	25.83%	21.21%	16.60%	11.98%	7.37%	2.76%

As you can see, although the 20% equity/80% bond portfolio fared much better in 2008 than the 80% equity/ 20% bond portfolio, the 20%/80% missed a great deal of the bull market in 2009 that the

80%/20% captured. In the next chart, I have provided a listing of these very same portfolios along with their expected annual return and standard deviation. (As of 07/31/2012 us.ishares.com)

	Equity/Bond					
	100%/0%	80%/20%	60%/40%	40%/60%	20%/80%	0%/100%
1 Year Return	5.36%	5.75%	6.14%	6.53%	6.92%	7.31%
3 Year Return	16.29%	14.36%	12.44%	10.51%	8.59%	6.66%
5 Year Return	0.18%	1.47%	2.75%	4.04%	5.32%	6.61%
3 Year Standard Deviation	15.65%	13.09%	10.53%	7.96%	5.40%	2.84%

(iShares, 2012)

It should come as no surprise that the 20%/80% portfolio has a lower standard deviation than the 80%/20% portfolio or that the 80%/20% portfolio has a much higher expected annual return. Before I get too far ahead of myself, though, it makes sense to provide a thorough explanation of standard deviation. Standard deviation is a statistical measure. Essentially, it seeks to explain a set percentage of the data being analyzed. To be more specific, if you have a group of 30 random numbers between 1 and 100, standard deviation uses the average of these numbers and says that 68.27 percent of the numbers will fall within X (+/-) of the mean (average). That is to say that, on average, 20 or 21 of the 30 numbers given will fall between a range given by the standard deviation. That is one standard deviation. Two standard deviations will account for 95.45% of the data and three standard deviations will account for 99.73% of the data. This is all based on the assumption that the data follows a normal distribution or bell shaped curve. Following are some exact numbers for those who prefer to see specific examples as opposed to reading about something on a hypothetical level.

Series	Random Number (1-100)			
		Mean	63.3	
1	58	Standard Deviation	28.35	
2	78	Range	Low	High
3	9	1 SD Range	34.95	91.65
4	84	2 SD Range	6.60201	119.998
5	74	3 SD Range	-21.747	148.347
6	65			
7	97			
8	64			
9	64			
10	99			
11	26			
12	18			
13	13			
14	89			
15	98			
16	79			
17	5			
18	35			
19	86			
20	62			
21	91			
22	94			
23	63			
24	28			
25	82			
26	40			
27	73			
28	74			
29	76			
30	75			

(Random.org 2012)

29

In our example of random numbers courtesy of random.org, exactly 20 of the numbers generated fell within the range given by one standard deviation. We also see that 29 of the 30 numbers fell within the range given by 2 standard deviations, which is exactly as we expected (28.64 to be precise). The one flaw to our example is that I have limited the number to a range of 1-100 which standard deviation cannot account for.

Hopefully the explanation and chart above makes everything clear. The reason it is important to understand standard deviation is the frequency of its use in the financial markets. In finance, standard deviation is used to measure risk. The higher the standard deviation of a portfolio, the higher the risk associated with that portfolio. It makes sense that a portfolio, (portfolio A), with an expected return of 10 percent and a standard deviation of 15 percent is more risky than a portfolio, (portfolio B), with an expected return of 5 percent and a standard deviation of 7 percent. Therefore, portfolio A has a mean of 10 percent, 68 percent of the time you can expect your annual return to fall between -5% and +25% and 95% of the time you can expect your portfolio to fall between -20% and +40%. Portfolio B on the other hand has a mean of 5 percent, 68 percent of the time you can expect the annual return to fall between -2% and +12%, and 95% of the time you can expect the annual return to fall between -9% and +19%. The question you have to ask yourself is: are you willing to risk your portfolio losing 20 or even 35 percent in a given year or are you more comfortable assuming the potential loss of 9 to 16 percent?

Determining what level of risk you are willing to take on is critical in a strategic investment because the portfolio will be designed to meet those criteria for risk and reward as closely as possible. More importantly, as a strategic portfolio, your allocation will not change as the market changes. That is why the second step of a strategic allocation is nearly as important. Creating a portfolio of non-correlated assets helps smooth out the peaks and valleys in the market. As one asset class experiences a fall, another asset class will experience a bull run, counterbalancing one another. The ultimate goal being long term gains with as smooth a ride as possible in the short term.

As you might expect, this form of investment dramatically loses popularity as market volatility increases. Very few people have the nerve and wherewithal to sit by and watch their portfolio lose money with the expectation that the market will eventually come back. Market volatility and fear have led to a new investment style known as tactical. The original concept of a tactical portfolio is not so different from a strategic portfolio. Step one: create a well-diversified portfolio balanced towards the investors risk profile. Step two, is where a tactical portfolio deviates from the strategic. Instead of sitting through the market, riding the ups and downs like a roller coaster, a tactical portfolio seeks to mitigate losses and heighten gains by shifting the overall allocation of the portfolio.

Think of it this way; say you are a moderate investor with a moderate portfolio of 50 percent equity and 50 percent bonds. A strategic portfolio is going to be 50/50 whether the market is bull or bear. A tactical portfolio might shift to be 65 percent equity and 35 percent bonds in a strong bull market or shift to 35 percent equity and 65 percent bonds in a bear market. Basically the portfolio seeks to increase risk and potential return when it makes sense to do so and reduce risk and, subsequently, expected return when the market is falling and you need to protect your assets.

Here I have used an example of a 15 percent shift between equity and bonds creating a total potential deviation of 30 percent within your portfolio. If this was the maximum the tactical portfolio could shift, it would be known as a tactical portfolio with a 15 percent collar. In other words, the portfolio could never be more aggressive than 65/35 or more conservative than 35/65. This is nice for someone who wants to protect their assets and take advantage of market swings but does not want their portfolio to deviate too far from their risk tolerance. You could also use a portfolio that can shift all the way to 100 percent fixed/cash and all the way back to 100 percent equity. This is sometimes referred to as a completely dynamic portfolio or unrestrained tactical portfolio. The advantage here is you can take complete advantage of market shifts and you can also completely protect your assets. The drawback is, what if the portfolio makes a dramatic shift, and does it at the wrong time. As a moderate investor you do not want your portfolio to shift to 100 percent equity right before the stock market takes a dive.

Whether the portfolio is unrestrained or has a collar, the premise is the same. You are relying on your financial advisor or a fund manager to determine when to make shifts in your portfolio. I will discuss the merits and drawbacks of this form of management in the final chapters of the book. For now, suffice it to say, that tactical management has rapidly become the investment method of choice. It's not too surprising either given today's market volatility and the promise of either outpacing the market, protecting assets, or some mixture of both.

Research

The demand for active, tactical management has also led to a new era of research. We previously discussed the extensive research that went on prior to a venture capitalist entering a business venture. Technology has made the flow and availability of information far more accessible than those early days. Analysts can use any number of websites to garner information about a company and the warrants of investing in that company. Requirements for reporting and providing annual and semi-annual reports means analysts can perform detailed research in a matter of a few hours, or even minutes, without ever leaving their computer or talking to a live person.

While technology has made it easier for analysts to perform research on a company, or multiple companies, in a very short period of time, market trends have also made their role far more demanding. The role of each individual strategist has changed from that of analyzing an entire portfolio to analyzing minute market niches. For example, a single analyst might be focused on small cap, value, domestic equity. Despite, or, perhaps due to, this narrowed focus, the analysts find themselves in ever increasing demand. As investors seek more and more active management, fund managers push their analysts to find the latest and greatest investments. Active research and active trading is no longer frowned upon, but viewed as a necessity. People want investments that will get them out of the market just as the bear pulls that market down and will get them in just as the bull begins to raise its head.

Analysts are not looking for long term investments as a venture capitalist once did. Companies are the talk of the Street one day and thrown to the curb the next, all on a murmur of a market swing in one asset class or another. Short term investing reigns supreme as managers seek out safe havens and the next Google. So what is the overarching theme? What are these managers and analysts looking for? It all depends on the funds focus. The overarching goal, though, is to time the market. The manager who perfectly times the next bull or bear run is king for a day...maybe even a week, until tomorrow brings a correction and a new trend, crowning yet another manager supreme.

The drawback is exactly what you might expect. Sure it sounds easy to predict when the market will start trending up or when a correction is about to hit and we are due for a pull back. Looking back at historical pricing it seems obvious when the last two bear markets were going to hit. But how many people actually predicted either of the last two bear markets? How many people actually acted on their own predictions? And how many people predicted both? The answer is startlingly few. Managers have been able to predict many moves, some even fairly frequently, but few, if any, are able to predict the market trends with any consistency over any length of time. Yet this is exactly what you are paying them to do.

You are paying them to make active trades that cost you money in an attempt to preserve your money. These trades are becoming more and more frequent and more and more costly to your portfolio. Once investments were designed to be held for ten or more years. Today, fund managers look for investments for the next quarter or the next few weeks, not the next few years. Even shorter term investment strategies are very common. People have looked for arbitrage opportunities, (mispricing), in the markets since the beginning of investing. In the past this meant reading the news earlier than your peers and being able to take advantage of your knowledge of a buyout, a natural disaster, a disruption in supply, a new technology, a new innovation or some other market action. Today it involves identifying mispricing between two or more exchanges offering the same security.

Today, the vast majority of securities transactions are made possible by any one of several exchanges, the New York Stock Exchange, the Chicago Mercantile Exchange, etc. Although, the exchanges typically do not take place at a physical location, but, rather, electronically. This allows for the quick and nearly seamless transfer of funds and securities. The way these exchanges make money is by acting as either a broker or a dealer for a transaction. Exchanges typically make money by offering the same security for sale at a slightly higher price than they are willing to buy it for. For example, TD Ameritrade offers a trading platform in which they search multiple exchanges for the best purchase and sale price. As I am writing this, the best price the exchanges are selling Microsoft Corp Com (MSFT) for is $26.94, (that is the ask, or price the exchanges are willing to sell shares of MSFT to me for), and the best price the exchanges are buying MSFT for is $26.93, (that is the bid, or price the exchanges are willing to buy shares of MSFT from me for). You will almost always see the ask price be slightly higher than the bid price because that is how the exchange makes its money. This is referred to as a spread. The more narrowly traded a security, the larger the spread, whereas a heavily traded security like MSFT has a very narrow spread of only $.01.

Where arbitrage opportunities come into play is if there is mispricing between one or more exchanges. This means, for example, the New York Stock Exchange has an ask price of $26.94 and a bid price of $26.93 for MSFT, but the Chicago Mercantile Exchange has an ask price of $26.97 and a bid price of $26.96. An astute investor would be able to buy MSFT from the New York Stock Exchange for $26.94 and sell them to the Chicago Mercantile Exchange for $26.96, making an instant profit of $.02 per share. This may not seem like a large profit but today's techies are utilizing super computers that are capable of updating prices on thousands of securities faster than the exchanges themselves and they are taking profits on price discrepancies of little more than 1 tenth, or 1 thousandth of a penny. However, they are trading such large sums as to make these miniscule profit margins very fruitful.

This form of arbitrage has become more and more difficult over the years with enhancements in technology. Where before an individual could have a friend watch the ticker tape at one exchange while he watched the ticker tape at another and place trades on mispricing over a few minutes span, today's mispricing typically occurs for such insignificant fractions of a second that only the fastest computers are able to pick up on them. This is market efficiency at its best.

Mispricing at this level is a very unique strategy, though, and is not commonly part of the average investor's portfolio. More common is the form of mispricing individual analysts are looking for. As previously mentioned, investors are utilizing active fund managers in an attempt to beat the market. The companies operating these funds not only rely on the expertise of a highly paid fund manager, but reinforce his investment strategy with analysts. These analysts focus on a particular segment of the market. Within that segment they are looking for perceived mispricing as opposed to actual mispricing, as in the previous exchange example.

An analyst might focus on individual companies, looking for mispricing of a particular company relative to its peers or relative to its intrinsic value. In the first case, the analysts might be following the healthcare industry and notice that many insurance companies are making massive gains due to a favorable change in healthcare reform. If one, or several, companies were participating in the gross benefits of this reform but their stock price had not reflected the rise in profitability, this would be a buying opportunity. Provided those insurance companies that still had relatively low stock prices still had strong fundamentals and good prospects of remaining profitable into the future, the analyst would seek to take advantage of this mispricing between a select few companies and their industry peers.

In the second case, an analyst would be looking at one company's fundamental financials such as their financial ratios, income and balance sheets, or even the trends of the stock price to determine mispricing. One such financial ratio is the P/E or price to earnings ratio. The P/E ratio measures a company's profitability relative to the price being paid for the company's stock. Commonly P/E ratio's range around 18. During the peak of the market near the end of 1999 and early 2000, it was not uncommon to see P/E's well over 30, 50, or even higher. Based on the P/E ratio alone, an analyst would typically consider P/E's over 25 or 30 to be high and possibly overpriced, where as a P/E's closer to 12 or lower would be considered low and possibly a good buying opportunity. Of course many other factors come into play. Average P/E ratios vary by industry, and P/E alone cannot tell you if a company is potentially a good or bad investment. Although a low P/E, relative to industry peers, could suggest that a company's stock is underpriced, it could also mean that the company is facing financial hardship and is going out of business. It is up to the analyst to use their expertise and the rest of their seemingly endless resources to determine which scenario is the most likely for the particular company being evaluated.

An analyst might also focus on the industry as a whole or on a regional basis. For the sake of continuity, let's continue our examples with the healthcare industry. Depending on the outcomes and decisions of the Obama administration revolving around healthcare reform, an analyst may recommend to over or underweight the entire industry within a fund's portfolio. Similarly, if a hurricane were to hit a major supplier of healthcare supplies in the US, this might be cause to underweight the US region for healthcare, at least for a short time until the supplier is able to begin distributing again or until an alternate supplier is found.

Despite massive efforts made by the financial industry to tailor investment products to the high demand for market timing products, individual investors still seem to feel the need to trade on their own behalf. Even those investors already in a tactical fund often sell their position after a major downturn has occurred, instead of relying on the manager they hired. The irrationality of the financial market has proven inexhaustible.

The Herd Effect

Rather than employing the logical buy and hold strategic, strategy or relying on the active manager that investors hire, they let their emotions get the best of them. As long as the market is cruising along in an upward trend, portfolios sit happily idle. Investors do not seem to care what is going on in their portfolio or what they are invested in. They know they are making money and that is enough. They certainly would not want to make a change during the height of that bull market. How could anyone possibly suggest that the bull has run out of steam, it is time to take your profits, let the natural correction run its course, and possibly miss out on the absolute peak of the market? If anything, now is the perfect time to buy.

On the flip side, in a down trending market the typical investor thinks the world is ending. They want to know what is happening to their account on a daily basis. They start showing concern after the initial correction and the bear has already taken hold of the market. By the time the bear reaches his full stride the average investor is seriously thinking about getting out of the market. It is not until the bear has almost tired itself out that investors have reached their wits end and act on all of their fears. So they get out, at, or near, the bottom of the market.

Traditionally, the act of buying higher and selling low has led to the gross discrepancy between the average investor's returns and the S&P 500.

How is it, with all of these tactical options available to us, a simple buy and hold strategy in the S&P 500, could outperform the investing public? The answer is precisely that concept posed above. Investors are initially very skeptical of a bull market and wait to make sure it is going to continue in the upward trend. Eventually, they see other investors making lots of money and they really think about getting in. Finally, confidence overwhelms them and they get in, at or near the top of the market. They make a little bit of money and share in the euphoria of the raging bull market for a short time until the inevitable correction occurs. At first, they view the correction as just a blip in the general upward trend and do not think much of it. After a while, the downward trend becomes clear and the investor is a little nervous but still has faith the market will return. Later, they realize the market is not coming back yet and they just cannot take another hit. So the investor gets out, at or near the bottom. Sadly, the cycle starts anew from there. And that is why the S&P 500 is able to outpace the average investor.

If you think these two trending markets sound bad, how do you think most investors react during truly volatile markets when there is not even a trend to follow? Even the experts do not know what to expect and find themselves acting on whims, shooting from the hip, going with their gut, and generally defaulting to whatever the general market feels is acceptable at the time. Now when I say, at the time, I am referring to a week or a couple of days, since the feelings of the market are so susceptible during these volatile times.

It seems in any market extreme, whether it be a rapid run up, a quick pull back, or a dramatic whipsaw between the two, no one is capable of independent thought. No one is capable of leading the horse to water when the heard is running the opposite direction. The reality is not that no one is capable, but that no one is willing. Who wants to be the one who predicts the worst market since the great depression? Even worse, who wants to make that prediction and be wrong? Yet again, what fund manager is going to risk jumping back into the market with both feet only to have her firm footing swept back out from under her by another decline?

In the end, everyone is drawn in by the concept of strength in numbers. It's like playing follow the leader, but the leader has no idea where he is going. Truthfully, you would probably be better off doing the exact opposite of the general consensus. This is a contrarian investment style and is not for the faint of heart. Even this strategy has its flaws. Few have the strength to ignore their friends, family, advisor, and the media when everyone is pointing at you and laughing because you are missing out and have made the wrong decision, or at least it looks like you have made the wrong decision for a time. Now that we have mentioned the media though, let's take a look at just how it affects the market.

The Role of the Media

Media for Investment Advice

We have previously discussed all of the detail and time invested in researching investment strategies. Early on, this in depth research was performed by the individual investor. Today, only an elite few are deemed investment gurus and the rest of the finance industry strive to make the right decisions and find the next big winner. The average investor has dropped out of this race to be the best and the brightest investor entirely. The idea of performing one's own research is not only completely foreign, but distasteful, in its entirety.

Instead, today's investors absorb their investment advice much the same way they absorb everything else; by watching or reading the news. Do not get me wrong, the news is great for tid bits of information and staying on top of daily happenings. The news provides weather reports, information on presidential candidates, events happening around the world that we would otherwise have no information on, and endless other benefits.

Using the media for you investment advice, though, means you are making a lot of assumptions. You are assuming the media knows or cares about the financials of the companies you invest in, that they have taken the time to research the potential effects a particular piece of news should reasonably have on these companies, and that the media knows your background, circumstances, and personal investment goals. In short, you are assuming the news has a greater motive than simply reporting the news and making a profit. While there may be a select few cases where reporters are seeking the betterment of humanity through their reporting, this is not the overarching goal. And no matter how strong a proponent to this cause, reporters still do not have the necessary background to offer investment advice.

There is a reason every show, broadcast, or article that publishes opinions on investments has an extensive disclosure at the end. Perhaps the following words sound familiar:

> "The performance data quoted above represents past performance. Past performance does not guarantee future results and principal value will fluctuate so that an investor's shares, when redeemed, may be worth more or less than their original cost. Current performance may be lower or higher than the performance information quoted.
>
> Stock investing involves risk including loss of principal. Securities of small companies are often less liquid than those of large companies. As a result, small company stocks may fluctuate relatively more in price. International and emerging market investing involves special risks such as currency fluctuation and political instability, and may not be suitable for all investors. Bonds (fixed income) are subject to market and interest rate risk. Bond values will decline as interest rate rises, issuer's creditworthiness declines, and are subject to availability and changes in price." (Loring Ward 2012)

Pay close attention to these words. All too frequently this disclosure is glossed over with hardly more than a cursory glance. No one likes to read the fine print, but these are words to live by. Your financial soundness may depend on it.

Take your own situation into account. If I say to you, buy XYZ as it's sure to double in the next 6 weeks, what does that mean to you? For some this could be a great investment opportunity. For others, this particular investment could be far too risky because I did not bother to tell you that there is a 25 percent chance the company will go belly up in that same time frame. Or maybe you are in a 38 percent tax bracket and the short term gains would only serve to increase your tax liability at the end of the year. The point is, it does not make sense to act on information when presented in such a limited scope.

Jim Cramer of Mad Money has only a couple of minutes to present on any one investment. The Wall Street Journal rarely uses more than a few paragraphs to share their opinion on a company. These are often highly regarded investment sources. Neither of them provide you with a prospects or an annual report though. Nor do they ask you about your current investment experience, financial situation, or retirement needs. How do you expect to garner valuable investment advice when it is presented in such short form and never tailored to you?

Negative News

The media is famous for reporting on everything that is negative, outstanding, shocking, etc. because that is what sells. They have no incentive to report on positive happenings in any industry, much less finance. Slamming headlines like, "Worst Crisis Since '30s, With No End Yet in sight" (WSJ) demand your attention.

In the finance world the case is even worse. Positive news in finance provides headlines for a day. Negative news spawns hysteria, generate even more negative news, potentially for months to come.

Which headline do you think generates more revenue for the reporting firm? "ABC Company Reduces Chemical Waste From Its Chicago Plant by 20 Percent.", OR "The CEO of XYZ Reportedly Stole Over $22M From Employee Retirement Accounts." Ask yourself which newspaper you would pick up. It is not too hard to figure out why the news focuses on negative headlines given our insatiable lust for them.

If negative headlines are going to drive sales and, therefore, help meet revenue goals for the company, negative headlines are going to dominate the news. The same concept applies to any business. There are currently over 27 million firms in the US, of which only 1.5 million are non-profit. By and large, we are all in business to make money.

But what drives this morbid fascination with negative news in the first place?

Psychology of Negative News

Why is it important to evaluate the effect of the news?

Just so you know I am not crazy and overemphasizing the issues that the news causes, let us take a step back. I have read a number of studies that discuss the effects of negative news. More specifically, these studies related the effects of negative television news as opposed to newspaper or magazine news. However, I believe many of the same concepts can be extrapolated to print news to varying degrees. In any case, the applicability to print news may be inconsequential.

> "According to Roper (1989), 65% of those interviewed stated that television is their main source of news information." (Johnson 1996)

In fact, "…people may watch an average of 3 hrs of newscast weekly (Anderson, Collins, Schmitt, & Jacobvitz, 1996)." (Szabo and Hopkins 2007)

> "For many people, watching the news is a daily ritual that sometimes approaches an addiction. The elderly tend to be heavy viewers of TV, and watching

television is usually cited as the most frequently named daily activity among the aged (Davis & Kubey, 1982; Schramm, 1969). As for program preference, older viewers consistently list news and public affairs as their first choice (Bower, 1973)." (Johnson)

Is the news really negatively biased?

This is all well and good, and proves that the news is a prevalent factor in everyday life. Aside from our own intuition though, how do we know the news really is negatively biased?

"Television news directors are quick to argue that there really is a lot of crime and violence in the world and that it is therefore unfair to criticize them for doing their job in reporting it." (Johnson) They may even go as far as pointing out that despite the negative news in the world, when given a fair count, only about half of the news reports are negative. This may very well be the case and would seem to prove that the news really is equally weighted between good and bad. That is, until you account for the fact that not all news is good or bad, but neutral. Meaning 50 percent of the news is bad and the other 50 percent is neutral or good. The vast majority of the studies I have read seem to support this idea.

> "For example, Haskins, Miller, and Quarles (1984)
> reported that 60% of television news content could be
> considered as bad news in contrast to 22% that could
> be considered as good news in light of their analysis
> over a period of 3 months in the United States.
> Similarly, Stone and Grusin (1984) analyzed 1 weeks'
> worth of randomly sampled news on the three major
> commercial U.S. television channels (ABC, CBS, and

NBC) over a 20-day sample period. Across all three
channels there were significantly higher number of bad
news than good news, with 47% of all stories covered
being classified as bad news." "...using a phone
interview method Galician (1986) studied viewers'
perceptions of good and bad news. The results of the
study showed that three out of four respondents
believed the television newscasts are overwhelmed by
bad news considered depressing by 94% of
participants. About one third of the respondents
thought that bad news has undesirable effects on
viewers, and 59% believed that newscasts tend to
make things worse than they really are." (Szabo and
Hopkinson)

According to research conducted by Johnson (1996), "...slightly more
than half (53.4%) of all news stories depicted various forms of VCS
[violence, conflict, and suffering]." Similarly, "An average of 54.5% of
news time was devoted to VCS." (Johnson). What is even more
telling is the overemphasis of these negative stories. "On the
average, about two thirds of the news programs analyzed began with
such news [VCS] and 64% of the top five stories depicted VCS. Thus,
stations tend to emphasize VCS news by selecting these stories to be
presented earlier in the broadcast." (Johnson)

Even those in the news industry have openly discussed the
excessive reporting of negative news.

"In a special report entitled "America the Violent," NBC
anchorman Tom Brokaw asked whether TV news is
reporting violence or exploiting violence (Brokaw,
1994). Gabe Pressman, veteran TV news reporter in
New York, admitted that the glut of body-bag
journalism gives viewers much more violence than

they desire (Pressman, 1989)....Addressing the Radio
and Television News Directors Association, CBS
anchorman Dan Rather (1993) asserted that news
departments very clearly know the difference between
sleaze and substance, but that fear of ratings makes
them succumb to the "Hollywoodization" of the news.
News departments believe that violence sells and that
violence is what the public wants. Rather laid the
blame on media market researchers who dictate news
content. He called for more courage in the Edward R
Murrow tradition to resist such pressure, but went on
to admit that he often lacks it himself." (Johnson)

I think this leaves little question as to whether or not the media over
portrays negative news as opposed to positive news.

Why might this bias exist?

Once you acknowledge the excess of negative news, it is not
too hard to figure out why it exists. Simply put, entertainment sells.

When you think of wealthy individuals who do you think of?
Likely actors, professional athletes, musicians, singers, and comedians
grace the top of your list. All of these individuals provide
entertainment for the masses. And we are all willing to pay
handsomely for it.

Naturally, when profits, prestige, and ratings are on the line,
the media will resort to whatever sells best, and that is
entertainment.

"Former White House correspondent Don Oberdorfer
(1978) once warned about the selective nature of
television. News departments are not content merely

to report the news. Rather, they prefer to orchestrate "The Big Event." Today, Big News means Bad News. The pressures are enormous to treat news as entertainment and to make the news exciting. News gets packaged like soap operas, and there is urgency to create dramatic footage (Rosenblum, 1993)." (Johnson)

Does this negative bias affect us?

I think most of us would agree at this point that the primary task of the news is to make a profit and increase ratings. In order to achieve these tasks, the news must perform a balancing act. The most critical aspect of this act is to provide entertainment. In providing that entertainment, though, the producers recognize that viewers have only limited attention spans and, therefore, each feature is relatively short. So, too, must each feature be fairly simple to follow, or risk losing the viewer again.

It is not surprising that news media is tailored to be exciting, moderately fast paced and contains a moderate amount of information. According to research, these are roughly the ideal parameters for gaining and retaining viewers' attention most raptly. More specifically, our capacity for retention when presented with a positive message is greatest when the amount of information presented is low. As the amount of information presented increases during a positive message, retention tends to decline. When presented with a negative message, though, our capacity for retention is greatest when presented with a moderate to high amount of information. In fact, retention peaks during negative, arousing, (or exciting), messages that present a moderate amount of information. (Lang 2007)

It is my contention that the argument can be made that news media is presented in this very format. Geared toward being entertaining, arousing, and always presented with enough information to engage your attention, but without presenting too much information that could overload viewers. Intentional or not news media caters toward our retention of negative news.

To top it off, "negative things receive quick and thorough processing in order to protect the organism and positive things receive slower more deliberative processing to ensure the best choices are made." (Lang) So, not only are we more focused on the negative news, we are more apt to respond and react to it without thoroughly considering the choices and consequences.

Bare minimum, I think it is clear that we respond to negative news. The next question is how does negative news actually affect us?

How does this negative bias affect us?

"In general, the news of negative acts leads to greater personal attribution, whereas the news of positive acts leads to greater situational attribution (e.g., Jones & Davis, 1965; Reader & Spores, 1983; Wong & Weiner, 1980). Thus, we predict that a piece of negative compared to positive headline news would initiate a stronger tendency among people to make causal explanation. Negative acts deviate from norms or laws of the land and activate the prosecutorial mindset to restore social order (Telloch et al., 2007). Hence, we further predict that negative news would evoke implicational concerns as strong as the motive to make casual explanations." Causal explanations being defined by, "people...asking themselves questions such as (a) why did those involved in the event behave in the way they did? (b) were they basically good [bad] people? (c) were they under some kind of external pressure?" (Singh 2010)

As it turned out, their research supported their model of people as intuitive prosecutors. "As we noted, intuitive prosecutors are vigilant defenders of social order. Consequently they are less motivated to understand the world and more motivated to safeguard the fragile social order." (Singh) Here again we see that people react to, as opposed to first seeking to understand, negative news. Hence the rapid decline in the markets as more and more negative news is presented.

Possibly even more concerning is the lasting affect negative news appears to have on our psyche.

"A systematic investigation conducted by Potts and Sanchez (1994) showed that depression was associated with intensified negative feelings after viewing news broadcasts on television. Similarly, Johnston, and Davey (1997), using a pre- to post-viewing, within-participants research design, found that watching a predominantly negatively biased news program raised reports of anxiety and sadness that could subsequently increase one's emotional response to personal problems. Another, more recent, systematic inquiry by Harrell (2000) examined the effect of viewing positive and negative television news on various aspects of mood. Her results showed that those participants who have viewed negative news items reported significantly greater increases in anxiety and negative effects than those participants who viewed the combined or positive news items. Therefore, it is not surprising that televised reports of exceptionally negative events such as September 11th could lead to symptoms of depression, posttraumatic stress disorder, and general psychological morbidity in viewers (Galea et al., 2002)." (Szabo)

In their own study, Szabo and Hopkins found, "that a random television newscast triggers increases negative emotions manifest in heightened state anxiety and TMD [total mood disturbance] and decreased positive affect." (Szabo)

All of these studies seem to agree with Johnsons assertion that,

"The negative images on television tend to create feelings of danger, mistrust, intolerance, alienation, and gloom, or what Gerbner et al. called the "mean world of television." "The more people watch television, the more likely they are to have unrealistic fears accompanied by feelings of insecurity, suspicions, and hopelessness." (Johnson 1996)

Conclusion

If negative news has such a detrimental impact on us psychologically, and so impedes rational decision making, what options do we have? As it turns out, not many. In Szabo & Hopkinson's study they found that the negative effects of news media persisted in their control group despite being distracted, in this case by a lecture, for 15 minutes following the news broadcast. It was only through relaxation, meditation, and other stress management activities that anxiety and mood disturbance returned to normal levels. (Szabo 2007) Therefore, unless you have the opportunity and the determination to engage in some sort of stress management, like

52

meditation, for at least 15 minutes after watching the news, your best option is to avoid the news all together.

Downward Spiral

Now that you understand the psychology behind negative news, you know why it sells, and you know how it effects our decisions. Ultimately this results in a downward spiral that becomes increasingly difficult to correct. The spiral looks something like this.

ABC News Company publishes an article or broadcasts a report about XYZ company that sold subprime mortgages in the form of bonds. The subprime lenders defaulted on their loans and the bonds are now worthless. Of course, the company cannot support them either. Investors in these financial instruments freak out and liquidate their holdings. Investors reading the report are also leery of their own investments and many of them liquidate too. The market as a whole takes a small hit as a result of these liquidations. The news, in turn, brings out excessive numbers of reports about the decline in the market and how investor's confidence is beginning to wane. The waning confidence drives further liquidations and a bear market forms.

Next thing you know, companies cannot finance continued expansion and day to day operations because there are no longer enough active investors in the market. Growth slows, companies cut back production as demand stagnates, eventually they are forced to lay off a portion of their workforce to cut costs, unemployed families cut back on spending, driving the economy lower still. All the while the news is running rampant with stories of companywide layoffs, investor confidence is at an all-time low, and the market declines 30%. As always, the news was there to fill its role of hurting the economy and finances even more. At this point, those still in the market are either hysterical and can jump out at any point or are actively trying to take advantage of the market swings and failing miserably.

But what if, instead of freaking out about a segment of the market that had nothing to do with your GE or AAPL stock, you decided to turn a blind eye? What if the government stepped in to punish those that had created investments that should never have been offered to the investing public and ensure it would never happen again? I will tell you. The market still would have taken a small hit, but nothing in comparison to the hit it did take. There would have been little or no continued negative news to report on and, subsequently, read. The financial markets would continue on with only a slight blip. It seems hard to believe, but the only thing that drove the markets down as far as they went, was our own irrational behavior.

We are our own worst enemies. Our friends, our neighbors, acquaintances, and millions of people we do not even know. We are a collective body of irrational fools that the news feeds on. If everyone decided to invest just $1 tomorrow, the nearly $7B that flooded the market would almost double the average daily volume of the NASDAQ, NYSE, and many others combined. This would have a dramatic impact on daily trading, driving the market up far higher than previously seen on any single day. There is nothing rational about this subsequent uptick. Only your basic economics equation can explain the type of market movement just described. Supply and demand drives price.

It is interesting when you think about it, that something as simple as the balance between supply and demand is the building block for the financial markets. The value, earnings potential, or dividend payout of a company does not determine the price of their stock. Yes, investors use these measures to determine how much they are willing to pay for a share of stock, which does determine price. Ultimately, though, how everyone measures the fair value of a company's stock varies a great deal, because there is no one set method for evaluating a company. One analysis might use fundamental analysis, looking at price to earnings (P/E) ratios, cash flow ratios, and dividend yields, while another analyst might use only technical analysis, looking for trends in the stock price, or a head and shoulders formation. Between these two methodologies, or even within these methodologies, two analysts are likely to come to completely different conclusions about the same security.

All of these factors drive the downward spiral of the financial markets that I have referenced so many times.

Turn it Off

Turn it off! I cannot say it enough. Ignoring the news is not enough, so just turn it off.

On top of the negative news, what credibility do these reporters have? Do you want to take your investment advice from a journalist or a writer? Or from someone with a finance related degree and experience in the finance field? In fact, you should ask yourself why you are reading this book and what credibility I have. Stop taking things at face value and start asking questions. Be skeptical! If you take your investment advice from someone who is entertaining because they are loud and obnoxious, you might want to ask yourself what in the world you are doing with your life savings.

> "Stories are often episodic, ahistorical accounts that rely on stereotyped assumptions and fail to provide context or explanation. Instead of communicating substantive information that aids in understanding, television news often focuses on emotional and tragic elements that tend to inflame and even obscure what is taking place. Television news thus follows the same pattern of distortion found in entertainment programming." (Johnson)

The next time you see a headline like "S&P Downgrades U.S. Credit Rating for the First Time" that goes on to say, "The AA+ will push the global financial markets into uncharted territory...", ask yourself why. Why will this announcement affect my investments? What does this have to do with anything I own? In many cases, the answers are shocking. It probably does not have anything to do with your investments and it should not affect them.

Continuing with the S&P downgrade of the US treasury as our example, the only investors affected by this decision were those invested in US treasuries. Granted, that is a goodly number of investors. Even they were not really affected though. We are talking about the US government! All they have to do is restructure their debt or print more money. On top of that, this was a downgrade from AAA, the highest S&P rating available, to AA+, the second highest rating available and one most companies and governments alike can only hope to achieve. AA+ is still an incredibly high rating and is considered very close to a no risk investment.

Even more shocking was the surge of inflows, yes *inflows*, of funds to U.S. treasuries after the announcement. People actually invested more in US treasuries despite the downgrade. That tells me no-one was really concerned that the downgrade would actually have an effect on their investment in the US.

The equity market on the other hand, experienced incredible outflows and dropped precipitously in the two weeks leading up to the announcement as rumors of the pending downgrade spread. But why?

The fact is, any negative news in the finance world leads to heavy sell offs and these sell offs lead to further sell offs. One day, you see news about the financial trouble with Greece and Italy and how that can affect the rest of the European Union. Within seconds, funds, traders, and investors are acting on this news and selling their holdings. More often than not, the selling is not limited to holdings in Greece, Italy, or even the EU. Instead, investors, gripped with fear, sell their holdings in other foreign countries and the U.S. The next day, other investors see the results of the sell offs and sell their holdings as well. Next thing you know, the media is reporting on the massive sell offs in the equity market as a whole, instigating more sales. Somewhere in all of this unfounded chaos, the quant models trigger their sales, stop losses are hit, and the market has taken a 20 point hit in the span of two weeks.

Meanwhile, nothing has actually happened in the EU, no countries have declared bankruptcy or defaulted on their loans. In fact the rest of the EU has taken steps to find a solution to a problem that may never be realized. As for the Home Depot, Google, and General Electric, the debt issues in Greece and Italy were going to have little, to no, effect on their balance sheets. In fact, despite tough economic times they all have strong earnings and lots of cash on hand for future expansion and investments. But their stock still tumbled, just like everybody else. Not because there was any correlation to the original negative news that was reported on, but because of irrational behavior.

I said before, people do not do their own research. They rely on the news for their investment advice. Do yourself a favor. Don't even bother questioning the next news cast you see or article you read. Cut the hysteria off at the source and turn the news off.

Right to Know (Positive News and Supporting Your Country)

The media has continually hid behind the mantra of people's right to know. What about the people's right to know about the positive goings on in the world? Let's focus on the positive earnings, new developments, and great leaps in environmental sustainability companies are having. Let's put articles like this on the front page instead of burying them 10 pages deep in an excerpt that focuses on all the other concerns the company is facing.

Bare minimum, at least put things into context. Explain how the announcement actually affects investments.

If the media cannot muzzle itself, then maybe the U.S. government should. The finance industry is one of the most highly regulated in the United States. Financial advisors have a fiduciary responsibility to their clients. All literature designed to sell a financial product requires compliance review and record retention for several years. So, too, should the media be monitored. Although, it is not intended as such, newspapers, news stations, and websites are just as responsible for the "investment advice" they provide as a financial advisor. Any article or newscast is useless in regards to investment decisions in the absence of the proper education or the proper context. Still, the news is being used for investment decisions by those unable to understand the full scope and complexity of any particular announcement.

To a degree, I apologize for the harshness of this chapter. I do not agree with the untamed, overbearing weight of negative news in the media. I do understand that media is a business, however, and to stay in business they must sell. For some reason, unbeknownst to me, maybe we are all slightly sadistic; human nature is to tend towards that which is shocking, often negative, and heavy. The whipsaw action of the market today must come to a stop though. I see only two ways out of that; tame the people, or tame the news. Removing emotion from humanity is neither possible, at least not yet, nor acceptable. Therefore, the only option remaining is to limit the input driving emotion and the largest player of people's heart strings today, aside from possibly a significant other, is the media. Either turn it off or bring some equality to the articles being published.

Four Options

Avoidance

In the end you have a number of options when it comes to your investments: Avoidance, beat the market, take ownership, or seek dividends. Option one is to avoid the market all together. For some, this might be a reasonable option. If you have the money necessary to live comfortably in retirement and to achieve any life goals you have left, this is a feasible choice. Bear in mind, you also have to be comfortable watching the value of your money erode year after year due to inflation. Over the last several decades inflation has averaged 3.1 percent. An individual letting their money sit under their mattress, in a bank account, or vault earning no interest can expect the value of their money to depreciate at the rate of about $3.10 for every $100, every year.

Let's take a closer look at inflation. One way to look at inflation is to view the buying power of your money in years to come. In this example we will assume you have a nest egg of $450,000.00. One year from now that same $450,000.00 will be able to buy you $436,050.00 worth of goods today. Five years from now it will only be worth $384,442.51. Double it, in ten years, your $450,000.00 will only buy you $328,435.64. Double it again; in 20 years your money will only be worth $239,711.05.

Another way to look at inflation is to look at how much money you will need in years to come, to maintain the same lifestyle you have today. For this purpose, I will assume some pretty conservative numbers. We will use a 65 year old couple, who are ready to retire and are too afraid of the market to invest. Let us also assume that they have paid off all of their debt (mortgages, auto and other loans, etc.); the only cost they have remaining are that which they require for day to day life (food, clothing, etc.), whatever taxes they may owe on their property and vehicle, insurance, maybe a little entertainment, and some extra because you do not want to come up short. If I were to scale things back a bit, I could still live comfortably on about $35,000.00 per year. For a married couple, they will need at least 1.5 times that, $52,500.00. To maintain that same lifestyle one year from now, they will need $54,127.50. In five years they will need $61,157.91. This should be getting pretty routine at this point but let's go ahead and double it anyway and double it once more. In 10 years our hypothetical couple will need $71,243.62, and $96,679.10 in 20 years just to maintain their same lifestyle.

I think most people would agree that $52,500.00 per year is a pretty modest lifestyle. But in order to retire and maintain that lifestyle for 20 years into retirement, (assuming you are not going to invest and are forgoing all potential interest), you would need $1,372,632.33. I do not know too many people who have $1.4M stashed away just for retirement. And of those who do have this kind of money, most are not looking for a $52,500.00 a year lifestyle. This tells me, those individuals who actually have the choice of avoiding the market all together, are few and far between.

Well, if avoidance is not an option, what is?

Beat the Market

A second option is to try to beat the market. We have already discussed the idea of beating the markets ad nauseum in previous chapters. Just in case you did not fully understand it the first time, let's review it some more. As you can probably tell, I am not a huge proponent of active, tactical management. There is very little proof of its merits as few managers have been able to beat a simple index over any length of time. However, I will do my best to remain objective for the next couple of paragraphs to examine the merits and faults of active management and market timers.

First, the merits. Conceptually, timing the market is a fabulous idea. If one could invest in equities exactly at the bottom and pull ones investments out, putting everything into bonds, cash, or some other fixed income security just when the market peaked, one would have no worries and would also be filthy rich. I doubt anyone has had this experience, otherwise the world would know about it in a hurry. Instead, what we have seen is about what a rational investor would expect.

As an active manager your primary goal is to keep the investors invested with you and that requires keeping them happy. The number one way to make an investor unhappy is to lose their money. Not making them enough money is the second way, but it is a very distant second. If the number one way to lose a client is to lose their money, the fund manager is going to be conservative by nature. It is the fund manager or financial advisor that takes a bullish position just before the market tanks that is going to be fired. Missing a portion of a bull market may receive some groans from the peanut gallery, but chances are, you will still have a full bag of peanuts. Hence, the expected returns. Active fund managers tend to perform better during a bear or volatile market but tend to lag during a bull market. This has also led to most active managers lagging the indexes over the long term.

I should also note here that the indexes most active fund managers are benchmarked to cannot actually be invested in. Say, for example, an active manager uses the following benchmark; 50 percent S&P 500, 30 percent MSCI EAFE, and 20 percent Barclays Capital Aggregate Bond Fund. The drawback is, no one can actually invest in this index directly and receive the same returns that these indexes quote. You or I could go out tomorrow and create a portfolio that fits these criteria exactly. You might choose to use iShares, due to their low cost structure, in which case, your portfolio would consist of 50 percent IVV, 30 percent EFA, and 20 percent AGG. For example, had you looked at this portfolio based on the indexes in 2011 you would have calculated a return of -1.02%. However, if you had actually invested in these ETFs your realized performance would have been closer to -1.24%. But why is there a discrepancy? (iShares 2012)

First off, there are trading costs. Not just your trading cost for buying each of these indexes, but also the trading costs iShares has to buy shares of all of the companies represented in the index. The indexes iShares creates also tends to drift a little as time passes. Over the months, companies tend to be added to an index as other companies fall out. In order to keep trading costs to a minimum, iShares, like most ETF managers, will not trade every time a company is added or dropped. Instead, they will probably rebalance the portfolio every six months or every year to match the index. On top of that, and despite being one of the lowest cost ETF fund families, iShares still has to make money too.

So you can see why the benchmarks active fund managers compare themselves to, really are not fair. An actual investment in one of these benchmarks would nearly always perform worse than the benchmark itself. Unfortunately, even with these additional costs added in to drag down the benchmark, most active fund managers still underperform over the long term.

The one great advantage to an active investment style is continuity. Yes, an investor would have done far better over the long term had they simply bought and held a well-diversified basket of equity securities. Unfortunately, most investors did not have the stomach to ride through the web of fantastical media and discombobulated markets. Instead, most investors followed the herd, buying in when the market was already high, and selling out when the market had already progressed through most of its fall. As a tactical manager, your job was to take advantage of these wild swings. In reality, tactical mangers just attempt to mitigate the extremes. The benefit is that more investors are able to emotionally tolerate the more moderate swings of many tactical managers and are able to, therefore, stay invested.

The benefits of staying invested can be exponential. If you do not believe me, refer back to the chapter on the herd effect and how the average investor has grossly underperformed the S&P 500 index.

Ownership Part Two

Better yet, take ownership of your investments. Know what you are investing in and why. This does not mean going to your advisor and taking their word for it. Nor does it mean listening to Jim Cramer and doing what he or any other media source says even if you do understand it. Knowing what you invested in means knowing the general business of the companies you are invested in. You should know what drives revenue and the bottom line of each of your investments. Without this knowledge you cannot take the next step of understanding what factors could actually affect your investments. Understanding these factors is a critical step, too. Sure, you probably know very well that Apple (APPL) makes the majority of its money from selling computers, but how much do you know about their suppliers? What do you know about Intel, Apple's processor supplier? Do you know how Apple derives the rest of its income? You probably also know that Toshiba and Dell are two of Apples competitors, but do you know what products they are designing, if any, that could take market share? What industry regulations could affect the technology industry? These are the factors that really apply to Apple, but most investors cannot answer these questions.

Most investors can, on the other hand, give you a detailed description about S&P's downgrade of the U.S. government and how that affected their investment decisions. Despite having next to no bearing on Apple's performance, the U.S. downgrade affected Apple's stock price, and the volatility of the entire equity market, far more than any factors that were actually related to the individual companies.

Once you understand what you are invested in, you must also know why you are invested in that company and what that portion of your investment really means to your overall portfolio. While individual investment should be strong on a stand-alone basis, the investments that comprise your portfolio should be even stronger when taken as a whole.

Certain stocks might be in your portfolio to provide a steady stream of income through dividends. You might get concerned over the fluctuation in price of these securities but the truth is, the price fluctuation really does not matter, provided the dividend is still paying out at the rate you require to maintain your current level of income. In this scenario, changes in the dividend payments are far more important than industry, world, or economic news.

Other stocks might be present to provide growth opportunities. These securities tend to fluctuate in price far more than other investments but also tend to outperform over an extended period of time. Guess what? If you let your emotion get the best of you and sell these types of securities because they have experienced a loss over the short term, all you have accomplished is realizing a short term loss on an investment that was designed to be held for the long term.

You may also hold bonds in your portfolio. Bonds can also range from relatively risky to very stable. In any case bonds tend to perform well in different market cycles from equities, (stocks), and therefore, might add drag to your portfolio during bull equity markets and bolster your portfolio when equities are experiencing a lull. Being too aggressive in bonds, though, (holding predominantly BB+ or less, "Junk Bonds"), can lead to a portfolio that is no more diverse than an all equity portfolio. Hence, the need for very highly rated bonds as well.

Provided investors are willing to take the time to learn about their investments and gain a full understanding of how outside events could affect these investments, the volatility of the market could be tamed. Realistically, removing emotion from the market is impossible. Curbing the fear that drives the market is feasible, though. All it really takes is a commitment to your investment. Commitment stems from what is being invested. If an individual has invested no time into their investment decisions and only their money, they are going to be all too willing to change those investments at the slightest sign of uncertainty. However, if an investor takes time to investigate and fully understand their potential investments, the chances of that investor swapping to a new investment are much slimmer. Not only have they dedicated a great deal of their own time to the original investment, they would also have to dedicate an equal amount of time to a new investment.

I am not saying people should take time to research their own investments just because of the benefits to the markets either. A well thought out investment strategy and well-researched investments lead to greater gains for the individual investor as well. If you have not read, "Lesson's from the Legends of Wall Street," by Nikki Ross I highly recommend it. Nearly all of the Legends of Wall Street reviewed in the book have one thing in common: their investment time frames. Warren Buffett typically held stock in a company for 10 years, as did his investment company, Berkshire Hathaway. Thomas Rowe Price also advocated investing for the long term.

These gurus in the investment world did not just hold onto these securities for the long term because they thought a long term buy and hold strategy was the right method to invest. They held on because they had put enough time and research into their investments that they knew when a market event was really significant enough to warrant a sale of their holdings. More importantly, they also knew how the normal ups, downs, and sometimes rapid corrections, would affect their holdings and did not get overly concerned by this market volatility.

These are just a few of Warren Buffett's success stories.

Company	Invested	Value 1999 (Not necessarily sold)
Wells Fargo (1990)	$392 Million	$2.39 Billion
Washington Post (1974)	$10 Million	$960 Million + $7 Million in Dividends
Coca-Cola (1987-88)	$1.3 Billion	$11.65 Billion

(Ross 2000)

As you can see, all of these investments were held for 10 years or more. If the professionals are not trying to time the market and are not trading on whims, why should you?

This is not to say that you should simply buy and hold a grouping of securities and remain oblivious to what you are investing in. Quite the opposite. Ignorance is not bliss in the investment world. Ignorance breeds fear in the face of volatility and irrational behavior. So, do your research. Know what you are investing in and why, so that you can be comfortable holding it for the long term. And shut out the news! The news and media knows far less about your investments than you do so why should they guide your investment decisions. The news serves two purposes: making money for itself, which involves reporting on that which is shocking and grotesque, and stimulating more fear and irrational behavior.   Determine the best investment approach for you, determine the best investments to meet your goals and criteria, and, occasionally, rebalance or adjust that portfolio to keep it in line with your goals. Do not let the media and the herd effect get the better of you.

Dividends

A second successful approach to investing is investing for dividends. Now, this is not really a whole new approach to investing. Taking ownership of your investments is really the first step to a successful investment. Having a dividend focus is simply an extension of ownership with a specific strategy.

Before I get too far ahead of myself, though, let me explain why you might want to focus on dividends within your investments. Consider the S&P 500 and the lost decade. From 2000 to 2009 the S&P started at $1,320.28 and ended at $1,115.10. This represents a return of -1.67% annually, but it does not include dividends. If we were to include the payout of dividends in our assessment, the S&P would have returned -0.95% annually over the very same time period. This is a total return of 0.72% from dividends alone. While this does not quite get us into positive territory, it makes a big difference when you consider a $100,000 investment, which would only be worth $84,459.36 in the first instance and $90,880.42 after including dividends. If you are not including dividends in your investment approach you are missing out on a large opportunity.

Another nice benefit to investors is the way dividends tend to smooth out your overall return. Think about it. If you are invested in

XYZ company, paying a 5% dividend, the stock would have to take a hit of at least 5% before your portfolio would be negative for the year. Furthermore, the hit the stock itself takes is an unrealized loss and may never be realized in your portfolio. The 5% dividend is immediately attributable to your net worth if you choose to take it as income. Better yet, reinvest that 5% dividend to purchase more shares of the original security. This will increase your overall holding, helping to bolster your net dividends down the road and is even more beneficial if the stock really has taken our hypothetical hit because your 5% dividend was able to purchase even more shares.

Furthermore, high dividend paying stocks are less susceptible to the swings of the general market. This can be seen to an even greater extent with preferred stock. (Most stock investors choose to purchase is referred to as common stock. Common stock represents direct ownership in a company, has voting rights, tends to have more upside potential, has the potential to be paid a dividend, and is the last to be paid back in the event that the company declares bankruptcy. Preferred stock also represents ownership in the company but it does not have voting rights, experiences fewer fluctuations in price due to the overall market and, therefore, has less upside potential, has the "right" to be paid a dividend, and is paid back before common stock in the event the company declares bankruptcy. When I say that preferred stock has the right to be paid a dividend, I mean preferred stock typically has a declared dividend so that investors know what to expect. Whatever this declared dividend may be, the preferred stock holders will receive their dividend before any dividend is paid out to common stock holders. In some cases the preferred dividend is also cumulative. This means a holder of a 4% dividend preferred stock could expect to be paid 4% over the course of a year, typically through quarterly dividends. On a quarterly basis, that would be 1% every quarter. If a company only pays out .5% in a quarter, the preferred stock holder could expect to be paid 1.5% [1% for the current quarter plus .5% for the previous quarter] before

70

common stock holders are paid.) The consistency of a high dividend paying stock, and even greater consistency for preferred stock, is what leads to the reduced volatility of the stock price.

If an investor had a good idea what they would be paid in the form of a dividend and the dividend is the primary reason for investing, the importance of the actual stock price is greatly reduced. A lesser focus on the stock price reduces the chance that people will buy or sell the security due to outside market circumstances. This in turn reduces the volatility of the stock itself and further reduces the focus on the price due to the lessoned volatility.

Depending on what you are trying to achieve, dividends may or may not play a part in your investment plans. For someone seeking income, dividends could play a very large role. For someone seeking to reduce the volatility of their portfolio, dividends may also play a role. However, for someone in a higher tax bracket, dividends may not be the best option. Currently dividends are taxed at 15% but that may change in future years. Keep in mind too, that the tax rate on dividends is substantially less than your income tax bracket might be; which is the rate your short term capital gains are taxed at.

In the End

In the end, your investment decisions must be based on your own circumstances, your income, spending habits, and ultimately your goals. Time and time again, I have advocated a buy and hold, long term investment approach. Clearly this will not work for everyone, particularly those who do not have a long period of time left to invest. For the rest of us, long term investing could most definitely be the answer to the hectic financial markets we are all bearing witness to.

Do not throw your money at a wall to see what sticks, though. Holding anything and everything, just because you hold it for the long term, does not make it the right investment. The reason buy and hold worked in the past and the reason buy and hold can still work today, is only partially due to the reduced volatility in expected returns. The real key to a solid buy and hold strategy, is the research done upfront. It is the painstaking effort put forth to determine the best investment for you.

There are too many investment options available to allow yourself to be satisfied with anything except the best. Finding the best is not going to be easy. Finding the best cannot be left entirely to someone else. Finding the best requires time and dedication to the search for your ideal investments. And finding the best, requires knowing yourself.

If the research I provided on the S&P 500 (short vs. long term investment horizons) and the investment strategy of Warren Buffett are not enough. Allow me to leave you with one final thought.

When an entrepreneur dedicates everything they have to their dream, they put all of their time, money, and resources into the success of their startup. Are they going to sell their dream to the first schmuck with a few bucks that offers to buy the business? Most likely, the resounding answer is no. For those that do sell to the first passerby, they get a pittance. Which is probably exactly what the company is worth at such an early stage in the business cycle. The real winners, the success stories we all talk about, are the entrepreneurs with the gal to laugh a million dollars in the face and turn the next several offers down as well to hold onto their vision.

The founder of Facebook, Mark Zuckerberg, was offered $75 million by Viacom only one year after creating the website. He was also offered $1 billion by Yahoo! in 2006. Every offer was turned down. While the value of Facebook has decline dramatically since it's peek and initial IPO of $114 billion, the company has still made its founder worth far more than the $1 billion offered by Yahoo!.

Google founders, Larry Page and Sergey Brin, were similarly offered $3 billion by Yahoo! in 2002. Despite the vast sum and the prospect of being financially sound for life, the co-founders were set in their resolve to see their business flourish in the manner only they had envisioned. Of course, the company is now worth nearly $200 billion.

Do not take this to mean you should never liquidate your holdings. Every investment has an expiration date. Whether you are ready to start taking income or you have found a better investment, a time to sell will come. Just do not be too antsy to bring that day about before its time.

Finally, remember these words from a very astute and favorite high school teacher of mine: "When it comes to investing, pigs get fat and hogs get slaughtered."

What to Look For

Honestly, if you have come this far in the book you probably already have a general idea of what to look for in a company. Specifically, you want a company that pays a steady dividend, has dividend growth, is likely to be in business for the long term, and with whom you are familiar. So let's begin.

When looking for a company with a steady dividend you should consider a couple of things. First, you want a dividend that is neither too high, nor too low. Too often, investors get caught up looking for high yield. Yield is the percentage pay out off a dividend relative to the price of the stock (dividend/price per share). Especially as investors transition into retirement, they begin to look for sources of income within their portfolio. One potential source of income is that derived by a steady payment of dividends. But be wary of those stocks paying an exceedingly high dividend relative to their price per share, i.e., have a high yield. This is usually, not always, but usually, a sign that the company is going to be facing tough times ahead. Few companies can afford to pay the majority of their earnings to shareholders, rather than reinvesting in the company and stay in business for any extended period of time. As a rule of thumb, I tend to avoid anything with a yield over 10% or at least limit my exposure to these holdings. With that said, there are a number of securities, REITs, Limited Partnerships, Oil & Gas holdings, that pay dividends that far exceed my 10% limit that may be great investments. For the purposes of this book, we will exclude any discussion of these types of holdings and defer further study to the reader.

Second, look for a dividend that has been paid out consistently over the long term. Long term, steady dividend payments are important for two reasons. One, companies that have paid dividends for many years, even decades, like Johnson & Johnson, are more likely to continue paying those dividends for many years to come, despite volatile markets. Speaking of volatile markets, one of the primary reasons for investing for dividends is to provide a more consistent return. If a company pays $.50 per share one quarter, $2 per share another quarter, proceeds to pay $0.00 for the next three quarters, and then comes back to pay another $.75 dividend per share, this will not help to reduce the volatility of your account. More to the point, further uncertainty will not help you stick to your long term investment strategy and you will find yourself back with the crowd, buying high and selling low.

Below are a couple of case examples you can use to get a better idea of what I mean by a steady dividend.

Company	Baker Hughes Inc.	Halliburton Co	Ross Stores Inc.
Ticker	BHI	HAL	ROST
Year	Dividend	Dividend	Dividend
2002	$ 0.46	$ 0.25	$ 0.10
2003	$ 0.46	$ 0.25	$ 0.13
2004	$ 0.46	$ 0.25	$ 0.18
2005	$ 0.48	$ 0.25	$ 0.22
2006	$ 0.52	$ 0.30	$ 0.26
2007	$ 0.52	$ 0.35	$ 0.16
2008	$ 0.56	$ 0.36	$ 0.20
2009	$ 0.60	$ 0.36	$ 0.25
2010	$ 0.60	$ 0.36	$ 0.35
2011	$ 0.60	$ 0.36	$ 0.47

(SEC 2012)

The next thing to look for is dividend growth. You are going to be looking for a company that is paying a steady dividend, but is also increasing the dividend. On top of that, you want the increase of that dividend to be steady as well. It all sounds very complicated does it not? Yes, and no. Yes, if you were to look at the dividends of thousands of different companies and plot their growth rates over ten years or so, this would become very tedious. Fortunately for you, you do not have to do this. Most trading platforms offer research tools that will provide the dividend growth rate for you. Or, worst case scenario, eyeball it. I am not advocating this idea as a primary solution, but you will very nearly come to the same conclusion that someone using a lot of fancy statistics would come to. All you are really looking for here is a general up trend in the divided year over year. But not too huge of an increase. Just like high dividend yields, huge increases in the dividend payout are typically not sustainable.

The above examples also provide solid examples of companies exhibiting steady dividend growth.

After that, you want to look for a company that is going to be in business for the long term. Unless you are selling stocks short, a strategy that should be reserved for only the savviest investor, odds are you are not looking for the company you are investing in to go out of business. This brings me to the next question. What qualifies a company to stay in it for the long haul? The real answer is, just like everything in investing, no one really knows. We can make some very good estimates, though.

Companies that are likely to be around for the next several decades have probably already been around for a decade or more. This increases the chances that they are not a fly-by-night trend. The dot com burst would be one case in point. Strong earnings and positive cash flow are also good indicators to look for. If a company does not have earnings, or their earnings are low relative to their peers, they are going to have a tough time paying their debt, let alone paying a dividend. Positive cash flow is really just an extension of the earnings concept. If a company has strong earnings but consistently has negative cash flow, they are using more money than they are making. For a growth investor, this would be of little concern. I, for one, prefer a company, especially in today's climate, to retain some of their earnings for later use or emergency needs.

78

Lastly, you want to be familiar with the company. First, this means knowing what the company's primary business and primary source of revenue is. Be honest, how many of your current investments can you state their primary source of business without having to look it up? Odds are, this comes to a very small percentage, especially if you have mutual fund, in which case, you probably do not even know what you are invested in. Yet, this is just the first step to familiarizing yourself with a company. Supposing you have had a similar education to myself, you have probably heard the phrase SWOT analysis enough to make you sick.

I am sorry to say, but that is your next step. You need to know a company's strengths, weaknesses, opportunities, and threats. Dig in and dig deep. You should be able to list several of the company's key advantages, places where they are weak, potential expansion or increases in production, and what their competitors are doing that could drag down their sales.

Start with the company's website and their annual report. Most companies make their annual report available on their website. This is a great place to get a feel for the internal operations of each firm. The strengths and weaknesses are those things that a firm can control. So too, is it a good place to form ideas on what outside influences could affect the firm. Think outside the box for this portion of your analysis. Listing the firm's competitors is just the beginning. You need to take the next step to figure out what regulations, trends, and environmental changes could also affect each company you invest in.

For example, we all saw how beneficial the iPhone was for AAPL. Will their next product have the same affect? How might enhancements in hybrid technology and all electric vehicles affect your holdings in oil refineries? What would happen to utility companies if the government set new requirements or new caps on the price charge for kilowatt-hours? These are the types of questions you need to be asking yourself.

You can see how time consuming this can become. Hence, the reason investing has become so disconnected from the original investor. No one wants to take the time to invest for themselves. Unfortunately, that is what we are going to need to do to stop the repetitive cycle of losing to market emotion. How far you take your research and to what degree you control your investment portfolio is entirely up to you. What I recommend is finding a balance that will allow you to get the best of both worlds, control of your investments, and retention of your free time.

Know in advance how much time you can invest in the research you are going to undertake. Once you have exceeded that limit, do not let your analysis consume you to the point of neglecting the other important aspects of your life. Know, too, the limits of your own financial knowledge. Having read this book, you may be very comfortable investing the dividend, income, and large cap value portions of your portfolio. On the other hand, you may still be shaking, while making decisions on what to invest in when it comes to emerging markets. Keep in mind that is not a bad thing. In fact, knowing your own weaknesses will be key to your own success as an investor. With that said, do not let your weakness get the best of you.

If you choose to leave international, bond, commodity, currency, or even some domestic portions of your portfolio to the professionals, do not forget, you still need to understand these investments. Talk to your financial advisor or do your own research on mutual funds and exchange-traded funds to ensure every aspect of your portfolio is taken care of. Furthermore, gain an understanding of these parts of your portfolio. I am not asking you to delve in to the same degree of research you may undertake for your domestic dividend focus. But if you fail to understand what you are investing in, and why, you will fall right back into the trap of buying high and selling low. Why? Because lack of education, guidance, or understanding leads to second-guessing, which leads to following the crowd.

In the process, do not miss these key components to a well-diversified portfolio:

Equities
   Domestic
      Large Cap
         Value
         Growth
         Core
      Mid Cap
         Value
         Growth
         Core
      Small Cap
         Value
         Growth
         Core
   International
  Large Cap
         Value
         Growth
         Core
      Mid Cap
         Value
         Growth
         Core
      Small Cap
         Value
         Growth
         Core
   Emerging Markets
   Alternatives

Commodities

        Metals/Mining

        Oil/Gas

        Goods (Salt/Sugar/Grains/Legumes)

        Wood

    Currencies

    Mergers & Acquisitions

    Private Equity

    Managed Futures

Fixed Income

  <u>Domestic</u>

    Investment Grade

      Government

      Corporate

    High Yield

      Corporate

  <u>International</u>

    Investment Grade

      Government

      Corporate

    High Yield

      Government

      Corporate

  <u>Emerging Markets</u>

    Government

    Corporate

  <u>Alternatives</u>

    Fixed Income Arbitrage

Cash Equivalents

  <u>Cash</u>

  <u>Money Markets</u>

Stressed yet? Don't be. This list is hardly all-inclusive or completely necessary. You will find most mutual funds and ETFs can cover multiple categories. Think of this as a hit list that will help you properly diversify your portfolio. Your goal is to have several investments in each primary category (Equity, Fixed Income, and

Cash). Make sure to have three or four investments in equity and ensure they cover both domestic and international investments. The same holds true for your Fixed Income investments, although you may need a few more or a few less holdings in this category depending on how much of your portfolio this actually accounts for. In terms of Cash equivalents you rest pretty soundly with a single, solid money market fund.

The one warning I cannot stress enough is do not let anyone fool you into thinking that gold is a cash equivalent. Sure, gold has historically climbed over extended periods of time and is negatively correlated to the market, so people use it as a hedge to market movements. The truth is, the price of gold and your investment can be just as volatile as any equity investment. Given how highly prized gold is currently and how often it is in the news, I would not be at all surprised to see gold take a sizeable tumble. Use gold as a diversifying holding in your portfolio but nothing more. I would never have more than five percent in my own portfolio and I would caution the reader to keep gold to no more than 10 percent, at the absolute most, within your own portfolio.

How to Get Started

Odds are you already have one or more investment accounts. They may be individual, custodial, or joint, qualified or non-qualified, trusts, or any number of categories. The important point is that you have them and if you do not, that you get started as soon as possible. Even if you just open up a savings account, stowing money away now is critical to your financial future.

Even if you already have one or more of the accounts listed above you will still find this section beneficial, especially if you are in need of consolidating your accounts.

Your first step toward achieving your financial goals is to determine what you are saving for. Are you saving for a major purchase in the near future, like a down payment on a house or a car or possibly even a vacation? Are you saving for college tuition for your kids or grand kids? Or are you saving for retirement? These are questions you will have to answer before you begin.

You will also have to determine how much you can reasonably afford to put away without harming your standard of living. In some cases, you may be able to put away a lot more than you think if you can tighten the belt a little bit and curb your, and your family's, spending habits. More likely than not though, you may find you cannot put away as much as you need to achieve your goals. Forward thinking and setting reasonable growth expectations will play a huge role in evaluating your savings needs.

The hardest part of investing is the potential for coming up short. This can happen one of two ways. Either the market was not favorable and you were not able to reach your growth expectations, or you did not put enough away. Setting reasonable growth expectations up front can help avoid both misfortunes. The growth factor that you use in your calculations will depend on the type of securities you invest in, which will depend on your risk tolerance and investment time frame. Given today's market, a reasonable growth factor may be as low as six percent. Although setting your growth expectation low means you will have to save more than you otherwise would have, it also comes with a great benefit. The lower you set your growth expectation, the more likely your investments are to exceed those expectations. If you exceed your growth expectations, assuming you have done all of your calculations correctly, you will have more money than you originally planned for and that is never a bad thing.

The other challenge I mentioned is not having enough money to invest to reach your goals. Your life situation and your personal financial goals, will determine what needs to be done if this is the case. If you have decided you want to buy a house or purchase a new car, for example. Not having enough money to put aside to reach these goals most likely means you need to rethink those goals, or at least tailor them back. Buying a smaller house, a less expensive car, or even postponing the original date you wanted to make this purchase is probably a better alternative than sacrificing your current standard of living. When it comes to retirement, though, the situation is altogether different.

If you realize you do not have enough money to stash away for retirement, serious decisions need to be made. Postponing retirement is one option, but even postponement can only be taken so far. As most people know, working your entire life is not only undesirable, but for most, impossible. For many people, ability to perform on the job tends to become more difficult with age. Of course, this will depend on the job in question and will vary from person to person. Realize, though, working forever is not an option for everyone.

In the case where postponing retirement is not an option, or even postponement will not suffice to reach your retirement goals, you will have to take a very close look at your current lifestyle and the one you hope to have once you retire. This becomes a balancing act, and one side of the teeter totter will have to tip in order to improve the other. Keep in mind too, the effects of compounded interest make every dollar you put away today more valuable than the dollars you put away tomorrow. The more you can save up front, the better off you will be.

Now let's take a look at how you can estimate how much money you will actually need to put away to achieve any one goal. Any good financial advisor should be able to provide an estimate of this sort for you. If you do not have a financial advisor, you should seriously consider the benefits strong financial advice can provide. In the absence of a financial advisor, or if you would just like to see the numbers for yourself, the following tables and explanations will help.

I like to use Excel for most calculations due to ease of use and accessibility. There are many tools available on the web that can also run the calculations we are discussing, but I prefer the reliability of my own work. If you do choose to utilize the web, dinkytown.com provides a number of very helpful calculators.

To get started, we will actually end up working backward. Later, I will show you how to work forward to see what you can accomplish with your savings based on how much you can save, but for now we will start with the end in mind.

Say, for example, you are saving for a car, or for a down payment on a house, for that matter. We will assume you need to save $40,000 in five years. This could be to buy a car outright, or to put 20 percent down on a $200,000 house. To figure out how much we need to save we could plug everything into one long equation. In order to allow for flexibility, we will use multiple cells within Excel so that we can change any single input, or multiple inputs, to see how it changes our required savings. For example, we might want to change our target amount, the time frame, expected growth rate, or frequency of savings.

Required Savings	$ 40,000.00	
Years	5	
Growth Rate	6.00%	
Frequency	12	Monthly
Periods	60	
Required Monthly Savings	($573.31)	"=PMT(B3/B4,B5,0,B1,0)"

The equation that I plugged into Excel is shown in quotes. You will not want to have the "" in your equation. B3 is referencing the growth rate, B5 is referencing the number of periods, and B1 is referencing the required savings. Note that Excel returns a negative number for the required monthly savings. This is just to reflect that the value is an outflow as opposed to an inflow. In this instance, you would need to save $573.31 per month for the next 5 years to have accumulated $40,000, assuming a 6% growth rate.

Now that we have the equation built out, we can modify the inputs to our liking. If we were to increase our expected growth rate to 8%, our required monthly savings would drop to $544.39 per month.

Required Savings	$ 40,000.00
Years	5
Growth Rate	8.00%
Frequency	12
Periods	60
Required Monthly Savings	($544.39)

Similarly, if we reduce the frequency of our savings to annually, our required annual savings would jump to $6,818.26.

Required Savings	$40,000.00	
Years	5	
Growth Rate	8.00%	
Frequency	1	Annually
Periods	5	
Required Annual Savings	($6,818.26)	

This is a very simple view of savings. A number of other factors come into play when really evaluating your savings goals. For one thing, you will never experience the same growth rate every single year if you are invested in the stock market. An individual bond or a grouping of bonds paying a set coupon rate can achieve the same rate of return year after year, provided you hold them to maturity. The stock market will fluctuate, sometimes widely from one year to the next. For this reason, we are looking at your average rate of return over your investment horizon. In this case, 5 years. The other consideration to take into account is inflation.

If you want to buy a car for $40,000 and use $40,000 for a down payment on a house, is that how much you are looking to pay today, or five years from now. If that is how much you are looking to pay today, you better be ready to pay a little more than that in five years. Historically, inflation in the United States has averaged 3.1 percent. Inflation is how much you can expect the price of goods to increase every year. Put another way, the value of your dollar will decrease by 3.1 percent every year. Kind of depressing, is it not?

Now that we know what to expect, let's calculate how much we should really be trying to save in five years. In Excel, type "Amount Needed Today" in the first cell (A1). In the next cell, (B1), type in the amount you actually need, (ex. $40,000). In cell A2, type "Inflation". In cell B2, you will type the percentage you expect inflation to average over your investment time-frame. This does not have to be 3.1 percent. In fact, if you are looking to buy a home, the expected increase in home values could be far greater or much less than three percent on an annual basis. In cell A3, type "Years". In cell B3, type in the number of years you are investing. In cell A4, type "Amount Needed Tomorrow". Finally, in cell B4, you will type your final equation, "=B1*(1+B2)^B3". [Note: You will find it easiest to use Excels formatting tools. For cells B1 and B4, use the Accounting Number Format or $ sign. For cell B2, use the Percent Style or % sign. B3 should default to the General Format, which is what you want.

Ultimately, your Excel spreadsheet should look something like this.

Amount Needed Today	$ 40,000.00
Inflation	3.10%
Years	5
Amount Needed Tomorrow	$ 46,596.50

Based on our calculations, $40,000 will put you far short of your shiny new car. Realistically, you could need $46,596.50 to buy the same car that cost $40,000 today, five years from now.

Do not stop there. Go back to your original equation. Now that you know how much you will really need to meet your future goals, make sure you recalculate your required savings. All you really have to do is change the amount you entered for your investment goal, which should be cell B4.

Required Savings	$46,596.50	
Years	5	
Growth Rate	8.00%	
Frequency	1	Annually
Periods	5	
Required Annual Savings	($7,942.67)	

Next, let's look at retirement. You can use the same equation you already built for our first car/house example. First, we need to figure out how much you are actually going to need in retirement. Typically, this number should be about 80-70% of your pre-retirement income. Step one, figure out how much you will need every year to live comfortably in retirement. This step should not be taken lightly. These could be the most important estimates you make in your entire life. The following form will assist you in making these estimates and including all of the potential cost you could incur in retirement. I always like to include a 10 percent additional buffer just to be safe. After all other calculations are complete, simply multiply by 1.1%. I also highly recommend having all loans, mortgages, and debt of any sort paid off prior to retiring.

Item	Monthly Payment	Estimate
Housing		
Mortgage/Rent		$ 1,269.21
Property Taxes		$ 194.31
Maintenance/Repairs		$ 174.59
Utilities		$ 353.62
Total Housing	-	$ 1,991.73
Furnishings		
Household Equipment: rugs, furniture, appliances		$ 230.22
Household Supplies		$ 75.94
Household Operations: dry cleaning, computer repair		$ 71.10
Total Furnishings	-	$ 377.26
Food		
Prepared at Home		$ 359.81
Eating Out		$ 280.16
Drink		$ 46.84
Total Food	-	$ 686.81
Clothing		
Clothes and Shoes	-	$ 184.09
Transportation		
Car Loan		$ 386.96
Gas and Oil		$ 216.69
Insurance		$ 97.41
Public		$ 55.41
Total Transportation	-	$ 756.47

Healthcare		
Insurance		$ 163.55
Medical Services		$ 163.55
Drugs		$ 50.98
Total Healthcare	-	$ 378.08
Other		
Entertainment		$ 250.65
Personal Care Products and Service		$ 56.75
Reading		$ 17.24
Education		$ 75.63
Charities		$ 202.24
Gifts		$ 164.59
Miscellaneous		$ 101.23
Total Other	-	$ 868.33
Total		$ 5,242.77
Total with Cushion		$ 5,767.05
Annual		$ 62,913.24
Annual with Cushion		$ 69,204.56

(Schoen 2012)

This is a sample budget only and should be used as a guideline, a starting point, if you will. The estimates are also provided as guideposts only and are best reflected for the year 2012. Furthermore, estimated data is based on information provided by MSNBC, updated for inflation. You should do your best to fill in the center column with your own data and include any additional categories prevalent to you and your family.

It is important to note how large an impact mortgages and loans can have on your required annual budget in retirement. If you had already paid off your house and your car, your monthly budget requirement would drop to $3,945.26 from $5,767.05. On an annual basis, this amounts to a difference of $21,861.44 ($47,343.12 down from $69,204.56). This can make a world of difference in how comfortably you spend your retirement.

You should also note that this budget does not take into account additional streams of income. If you expect to receive any money from Social Security, an annuity, a pension, or some other source, you will need to figure out how much these streams of income will amount to on a monthly basis and subtract them from how much you actually need monthly. The remainder is what you need to solve for. By the way, if you are ten or more years away from retirement, I would not bother factoring in Social Security at all. But that is another topic to get into another time.

Now that you know how much you need in retirement, we can build a calculator to estimate how much we need to save monthly to achieve our retirement goals. To be perfectly honest with you, these next calculations might prove easier if you were to use dinkytown.com. For the sake of continuity, though, I will show the diehards how to go about these calculations for themselves.

We have a series of three calculations ahead of us. First, we need to figure out how much we need to have sitting in our savings, investment, and retirement accounts when we retire. In other words, on the day I retire, how much do I need to have saved in order to generate $69,204.56 per year for the rest of my life? Second, we need to make sure the number we just solved for is accounting for the effects of inflation between now and that first day of retirement. Third, we can finally figure out how much we need to save monthly, quarterly, semi-annually, or annually in order to reach that savings goal.

Step one, we need to build one more calculator. In cell A1, write "Required Income". In cell B1, write in the actual amount you came up with, monthly or annually, from your budget calculation. In cell A2, write "Years In Retirement". In cell B2, simply put the number of years you expect to spend in retirement, (we are going to have to make a number of estimates). In cell A3, write "Frequency". This is how many times per year you will be taking the income you listed for "Required Income". In cell B3 put in "1" for annually, "2" for semi-annually," 4" for quarterly, or "12" for monthly. In cell A4, write "Periods". In cell B4, write "=B2*B3", (the number of years multiplied by the number of times per year). In cell A5, write "Growth Rate". In cell B5, you are going to have to estimate how much interest you expect to earn on your savings while in retirement. In this case, I have used an estimated growth rate of six percent. This is somewhat conservative but not unrealistic, given a conservative investment and today's market environment. I also subtracted out inflation of 3.1 percent, which will eat into my 6 percent growth (6%-3.1%=2.9%). For retirees, I would argue that anywhere between four and eight percent is a reasonable expectation for growth on investments in retirement. Less inflation gives a range of 0.9 percent to 4.9 percent. In cell A6, write "Required Savings". Cell B6 is where the magic happens. Write "=PV(B5/B3,B4,B1,0,0)".

Required Income	$ 5,767.05	
Years In Retirement	30	
Frequency	12	Monthly
Periods	360	"=30*12"
Growth Rate	2.90%	"=expected growth rate-inflation"
Required Savings	($1,385,544.12)	"=PV(Growth Rate/Frequency,Periods,Required Income,0,0)"

Therefore, a couple retiring today, who needs $5,767.05 per month, will need to have saved $1,385,544.12 in order to maintain this stream of income and keep pace with inflation for 30 years into the future. The biggest drawback to this calculation is the need to assume how long you will live into retirement. Based on a 6 percent growth rate and 3.1 percent inflation, after 30 years, your entire savings will have been exhausted.

For those that have some time prior to retirement, our fun with calculations is not quite over. Our second step is to take the number we just solved for, in this case, $1,385,544.12, and figure out how much that equates to once we are ready to retire. Say for example we do not plan to retire for ten more years. If that is the case, we need to save more than $1,385,544.12 because inflation is going to make our cost of living even higher. Fortunately, we have already built a calculator that does this for us. All you have to do is input the "Amount Needed Today", and the "Years", and the calculator will give you the "Amount Needed Tomorrow" (or ten years from now as the case may be).

Amount Needed Today	$ 1,385,544.12
Inflation	3.10%
Years	10
Amount Needed Tomorrow	$ 1,880,212.83

As it turns out, you actually need $1,880,212.83, if you plan to retire in ten years. It is a little bit depressing to see how inflation affects us, but your ten years prior to retirement has its upside, too. Yes, inflation is going to make it harder to reach your goal, but that same time will work in your favor as your investments accrue interest.

Next, we need to jump back to the first calculator we built. Our goal, remember, is to solve for how much we need to save monthly or annually in order to reach our required savings of $1,880,212.83.

Required Savings	$1,880,212.83	
Years	10	
Growth Rate	8.00%	
Frequency	12	Monthly
Periods	120	
Required Monthly Savings	($10,277.42)	

Hopefully, this looks familiar. All I have done is changed the "Required Savings" from $40,000.00 to $1,880,212.83, "Years" from 5 to 10, "Frequency" from 1 to 12, and "Periods" from 5 to 120. That is all well and good except now I need to save $10,277.42 per month. For most of us, this is probably not realistic. I sincerely hope, though, that if you are 10 years from retirement you have some sort of savings already in place. For our example, we will assume you have already saved $500,000.00. [Note: if you have already subtracted out alternative income streams from our budgeting calculations, do not count those as savings here or risk double counting them.] In order to account for the $500,000.00 we already have in savings accounts, we will have to modify our required savings calculator slightly. In cell B7, our original equation looks like, "=PMT(Growth Rate/Frequency,Period,0,Required Savings,0)" or "=PMT(B3/B4,B5,0,B1,0)". The only thing we are going to change is that first "0". When you look at the equation in Excel you will probably notice that this "0" is holding the place of "pv" or present value in the Excel formula. Guess what? That $500,000.00 you already have is the present value of your investments. All you need to do is plug and chug. Your equation should now look like the following, "=PMT(Growth Rate/Frequency,Period,-500000,Required Savings,0)" or "=PMT(B3/B4,B5,-500000,B1,0)". [Note: do not forget to put that negative sign in prior to the 500000. It is just one of those quirks of Excel.]

Required Savings	$1,880,212.83	
Years	10	
Growth Rate	8.00%	
Frequency	12	Monthly
Periods	120	
Required Monthly Savings	($4,211.04)	"=PMT(B3/B4,B5,-500000,B1,0)".

$4,211.04 should be a far more attainable number than our original $10,277.42. In all likelihood, though, you probably have come to the realization that you will not need $5,767.05 per month in retirement, in which case, your required savings could be substantially smaller. Or, if your lifestyle really does mandate $5,767.05 per month, you have probably already put away far more than $500,000.00. Whatever the case may be, you now have all the tools you need to gain a fairly accurate estimate of how much you will need in retirement, how much you need to save prior to retirement to achieve that income, and how much you need to put away monthly in order to reach that savings goal.

Financial Advisors

What about your financial advisor, though? Where do they fit into the picture and what am I paying him or her for? If the previous chapters have not already deterred you from doing all of this research on your own, read the next chapter called "Flying Solo" and come back to this chapter. If after reading "Flying Solo" you have come to the same conclusion that many readers have already come to, (that they have no desire to spend hours or even days evaluating companies and building out their portfolio), this chapter will help you determine how to choose a financial advisor. If on the other hand, you have read "Flying Solo" and you are emboldened by the idea of taking hold of your financial future, read the chapter again, determine what is the most important to you, create your investment strategy, modify it as you learn, but beware the temptation to try drastically new ideas that deviate from your strategy and offer outsized returns, and most of all, GOOD LUCK!

For everyone who is ready to take everything they have learned and apply it to their portfolio with the helpful guidance of a professional, read on.

When you first meet with a prospective advisor, do not be shy about asking questions. Think of this as an interview. The financial advisor is there to try and win your business. They are applying for the position of financial advisors for you. This is your financial future after all, so be inquisitive and do not be afraid to challenge them.

Just like when I described evaluating a company, so too, must you evaluate your financial advisors (FA). Here again, we will evaluate your potential advisors from both a quantitative, (the numbers), and a qualitative, (people and feelings), perspective. First, let's start with the quantitative reasoning.

The first thing you can do to screen your prospective financial advisors is evaluate their qualifications. To get started, there are several licenses your financial advisor should hold at a minimum. #1) Your financial advisor should have a series 6, series 7, or 66. #2) If they have a series 6, they should also have a series 63 and series 65. If they have a series 7, they should also have a series 66. If the FA does not have a series 66 or one of the combinations of licenses listed in #2, walk away now, the interview is over. This may sound harsh, but you need to be sure that your advisor can offer you the entire gambit of investment options, from individual securities and mutual funds, to third party asset management in both a commission based and fee based manner.

Before I continue I want to be sure you understand the reasoning here. If a financial advisor is only licensed to sell fixed annuities, what do you think they are going to sell you? It will not matter what your financial circumstances or goals are, all that will matter is that he sells you a fixed annuity. We all remember the old adage, "If all we have is a hammer, everything looks like a nail." The above licenses are your first step toward ensuring your FA carries more than just a hammer.

It is also a good idea to ask your advisor if they are insurance licensed. This license, coupled with those listed above, allows the advisor to sell life and health insurance as well as annuities. While all of these licenses are "must haves," it is still probably not a bad idea to ask them outright which financial instruments they work with. If they do not list, life insurance, fixed and variable annuities, mutual funds, bonds, stocks, and third party asset managers, walk away.

Now that we have satisfied ourselves that the advisor has all of the appropriate tools, let's get back to my earlier comment about commission based and fee based platforms. Commission vs. fees refers to the manner in which your financial advisor gets paid. If a financial advisor tells you that he does not charge anything, or that his services are free, walk away now and report him to FINRA (The Financial Industry Regulatory Authority) because he is lying to you outright.

In the first instance, a commission-based advisor makes money based on transactions. Every time you buy or sell a security, the commission based advisor makes money. These are the types of fees that are easily hidden and often pawned off as being free. To be clear, we will look at a few of the most common investment vehicles. If you were to buy a stock, there would be a trading cost associated with that trading. These trading costs commonly range from $10 to $50 per trade, but can be much higher. This means if you buy a portfolio of 30 stocks, the total cost of investing in the portfolio could be anywhere from $300 to over $1,500 and the FA gets a piece of that. These costs also apply if you sell some of those stocks to access the money or buy new stocks. For example, if you were to rebalance your portfolio just once a year to sell a portion of the top 10 performing stocks and buy a portion of the 10 worst performing stocks, you would have an additional 20 trades that year. You can see how these costs add up.

Next we will look at mutual funds. If you purchase an "A" share mutual fund, there is a front end load for investing in that fund. While front end loads do range, the most common is around 5%. That means if you invest $1,000 in XYZ mutual fund, you are actually only investing $950. The rest of your $1,000 investment goes to the fund and the FA, but mostly the FA. Not only will the FA receive the bulk of that 5% commission or load, they will also be paid around

.25% every year that you hold the fund in the form of a 12b-1 fee. Although that .25% is not immediately apparent as a fee, it is part of the internal expenses of owning that fund and internal expenses directly impact your performance. Lastly we will look at "C" shares. While "C" shares do not have a cumbersome front end load like "A" shares, the 12b-1 fee for "C" shares is substantially higher. 12b-1 fees for "C" share funds are commonly around 1% or even higher.

An alternative to paying your advisor on a commission basis is to pay them a fee. With a fee based model, rather than paying your advisor every time you make a trade or an investment, you pay them a percentage of your total account. There are several advantages to this type of fee structure. First, you will see the fee you are being charged, in plain English, on your quarterly or annual statement. Second, a fee based advisor is incentivized to help your assets grow. Commonly a fee based advisor will charge around 1% or maybe a little more, around 1.25%. If they are paid based on the size of your account, they are going to be paid more if your account grows and less if your account shrinks. Therefore, the advisor is rewarded when your account performs well and suffers along with you when your account performs poorly. Furthermore, they are not incentivized to trade just for the sake of trading, creating a conflict of interest, as in a commission based account. Third, you will not pay more to change your investment strategy or for needing access to your money (i.e. trading). Fourth, fee based platforms frequently give you access to institutional third party asset managers that you may not have access to otherwise.

Clearly, I am a little bit biased towards fee based financial advisors. This is not to say that you will not find many honest, excellent, commission based advisors, or that you should only use a fee based advisor. In fact, many advisors offer both forms of compensation structure. All the same, the items I mentioned earlier are things you should keep in mind. Which form you choose is entirely up to you.

Getting back to our evaluation, though, there are several other quantitative based factors that we can take into account. Additional designations can be a great indicator of which FA has the most knowledge. The following list is hardly exhaustive, but does give you an idea of some of the most common designations.

- CFA: Chartered Financial Analyst
- CIMA: Certified Investment Management Analyst
- CFP: Certified Financial Planner
- ChFC: Chartered Financial Consultant
- CFS: Certified Funds Specialist
- CLU: Chartered Life Underwriter

The CFA is by far the most advanced designation in the list and also one of the rarest. Mutual Fund Managers, Hedge Fund Managers, and most Analysts have CFAs. You will not find many Financial Advisors with this designation, but if you do, it is definitely a positive sign.

CIMA has become a common alternative to the CFA for financial advisors as it is not as difficult to attain, but is still pretty comprehensive. You may find more advisors with this designation.

The CFP is the most common designation among high quality FAs. It is more focused on planning for retirement and savings and does not go into nearly the detail on analyzing funds that the CFA does. I still feel the CFA is a superior designation, but you are more likely to find a FA with the CFP.

The ChFC is a common alternative to the CFP, but like the CIMA to the CFA, is not as comprehensive or as highly regarded as the CFP.

The CFS and CLU are more specific designations. These designations are not as well rounded as any of the others but they do provide examples of additional designations you should look for that can improve a FAs knowledge base.

As I mentioned earlier, this is not an exhaustive list. There are many other designations that FAs could hold that improve the likelihood that you are choosing a quality advisor. These are some of the most common designations, though. I would especially look out for the CFA and CFP. This is not to say that you cannot find a quality FA without any of these designations or that every advisor who holds these designations is going to be top notch. I am only suggesting that advisors with these designations are more likely to offer a truly holistic approach to portfolio management built on a well-rounded knowledge base.

Now that we have discussed minimum requirements in the form of licensing and some of the additional designations that improve your chances of "success" with an FA, we can shift our focus to the qualitative side of the equation. Again, qualitative reasoning refers to the human approach. This is both simple to explain and difficult to implement.

Where the quantitative side required a detailed description of various licenses and designation that you can quickly check off the list in practice, the qualitative side is very straight forward to describe, but far more complicated in practice. The qualitative evaluation you will have to perform when meeting with each prospective FA is a simple matter of likeability. If you like the advisor, stay. If you do not, walk away.

It really is that simple. There is no point in working with someone that you do not like or do not trust. I do not care how many designations someone has, it is not worth the stress and frustration of working with someone whose personality clashes with your own. Similarly, you may come across a FA that does not have all the glitz and glam of plaques on their wall, but with whom you immediately click, this could be a great relationship.

Here again you will have to evaluate your own judgment, or possibly have someone else evaluate it for you. If you have a history of jumping into relationships, of any kind, with less than scrupulous individuals, you may want to overweight the quantitative side of your analysis and put less focus on how much you like the person. Furthermore, you and your spouse or significant other should both like the person. If you do not have a spouse or significant other, it would also be a good idea to have a close friend or relative meet the FA to give you their perspective too.

Once you have chosen; how to work with your FA

Once you have chosen the financial advisor you want to work with, employ the knowledge you have learned so far and will hopefully garner from the next chapter "Flying Solo". For those of you who hoped the hard part was over, that you had chosen your financial advisor, and now the work was over, I have bad news for you, you have only just begun. Your goal is to stack all of the odds in your favor, not just some of them. To achieve this, you have to be an active participant in your portfolio decisions...without being too active. It sounds counterintuitive, I know, but you will come to understand my meaning.

If you were the owner of a professional baseball club, you would not choose a top manager and let him have at it, would you? Of course not. Sure, you are going to trust to his professional judgment. Why else would you have hired him? But you are going to have your say in things as well. You are going to be setting the budget and expectations for the club that your manager has to operate within. Having the right team is just the first step. The team has to practice and learn to work together. The coach has to develop a strategy and line up based on the team and resources available to him. These are all decisions that you will need to help make.

Have you ever seen the movie Money Ball or at least heard the story of the Oakland A's? If not, you should. It is a great movie. More importantly, hear is a very brief recap. The manager of the

Oakland A's had been strapped for a number of years with a very tight budget for payroll. He pushed the owner to expand the budget if he wanted to have anything close to a winning year because the budget was so limiting on the players he was not able to recruit. To put things in perspective, the Oakland A's budget was roughly 1/4th that of other professional teams. You can imagine how difficult it would be to build a team of top notch players when your budget for bidding on those players is so constrained. For this reason he was forced to come up with an alternative method of building a quality team, outside of paying huge salaries. With the help of a young man that was heavy into the quantitative side of the game, they were able to develop a strategy of picking up undervalued players at bargain prices, that could buy them runs, and subsequently wins.

I equate this strategy to utilizing ETFs, (exchange traded funds). ETFs are the optimal way to capture a segment of the market at the lowest cost possible. If you are looking to minimize your investment cost, individual securities are your best bet, but ETFs provide broad diversification within a market segment while maintaining a low cost structure.

Mutual funds on the other hand are more similar to the New York Yankees with relatively high costs, (a very large budget). The trade off, of course, is your ability to command top notch players. In this case, you are essentially buying access to professional mutual fund managers. The managers are also seeking to capture a particular segment, (or blended segments), of the market(s), while providing their own insight into which individual securities should be invested in and which segments of the market should be over and underweighted.

Before I continue allow, me to interject my two cents on ETFs vs. MFs. The obvious appeal to MFs is having a professional manage your money. Given the higher cost of using mutual funds you would expect to have better returns. Unfortunately, this does not seem to be the case. According to Standard and Poor's, if you break down the various asset classes you can compare the performance of active money management (most MFs) to passive managements (ETFs and index MFs). Looking at the period from January of 2003 to December of 2008 we break down seven different asset categories. Note that this does not encompass your entire portfolio but it is a good start.

Asset Class	Percentage of Active Managers that Beat the Index
US Large Cap	28%
US Mid Cap	21%
US Small Cap	15%
Global	37%
International	10%
Emerging Markets	24%
Short-Term Inv. Grade Fixed Income	3%

As you can see, there is not a single asset category in which active managers were able to consistently beat their respective index. In fact, the best any active managers were able to do was in the Global category and still only 37% of those managers were able to beat the index. Seeing as these professional money managers, with vast amounts of resources, training, and research at their disposal cannot do better than the general market, what makes you think you can perform research on these managers to choose the ones that are going to beat the index? It is really just a crap shoot. When you break it down, you have a 28% chance of choosing a US Large Cap manager that can beat the index, a 21% chance of choosing a US Mid Cap manager that can beat the index, etc. When you combine just these seven asset classes, your chances of choosing managers that can beat their benchmarks in all seven categories falls to .00023%. I do not know about you, but I do not like those odds. This is the very reason I settle for index returns and do not bother trying to choose professional managers to beat the indexes.

This coincides incredibly well with research published by Morningstar on the correlation between cost and returns. "In every single time period and data point tested, low cost funds beat high-cost funds." Since MFs are typically more expensive than ETFs, and usually by a large margin, we expect ETFs to outperform MFs. Between the findings of both S&P and Morningstar, you can probably see why I am a big proponent of ETFs. That is not to say that MFs are a bad choice. I just prefer ETFs in my own portfolio.

The real point I am trying to make is everyone has their preferences. Your FA is going to have their own ideas about MFs and EFTs, as are you. That is why you need to explain to your FA what you believe, what you are looking for, and why. They may try to convince you to go against some of your perceptions and preferences and they may be right in doing so. The important thing is that the end decision is yours to make and that you need to make a decision you understand and are comfortable with. That is why you are not hiring a manager and letting them have free reign. The second you end up in an investment that you do not understand or are not comfortable with is the same second you start making poor decisions with regard to your portfolio. Do not let this happen.

If you do decide to go the route of active management, there are several different methods to pursue this management style. By far the most common is for you and your advisors to construct a portfolio of mutual funds that is designed to be broadly-diversified. What you really end up with is, essentially, a strategic portfolio comprised of active and potentially tactical funds. Reason being, you are probably not going to, and should not, trade between these funds on a regular basis, but the managers of the funds themselves may swap out the underlying holdings regularly, (hopefully still within the funds mandates). The drawback is, you are still left with the scenario described above where you and your advisor are trying to choose those select few fund managers who will outperform the index.

A far better approach is to outsource this selection process to a third party asset manager, (TPAM). Take Russell, for example. Russell Investments is an institutional money manager. They manage money for groups like the Bill and Melinda Gates Foundation, Boeing and Coca-Cola's Pension plans, and General Motors. The fact that large institutions such as these trust Russell with their money is probably reason enough to invest with them. The method behind their investment strategy is far more moving, though.

Russell has over 20 offices worldwide and more than 500 investment professionals dedicated to manager research and portfolio construction. This allows them to evaluate the entire universe of more than 8,200 fund managers. Using quantitative research methods they narrow it down to 5,000 managers. Due to their vast amount of resources they have the ability to conduct 5,000 face-to-face meetings with these managers to further narrow the pool down to 600 that they will give a "hire" (buy) rating to. From that 600, roughly 200 will receive a position inside a Russell fund.

I do not mean to belittle the work of the well-qualified FAs in the industry. They simply do not have the time or resources to conduct the same level of research that a global institution like Russell is able to provide. The real point here being, if the odds of picking managers who will outperform is so slim, yet you are still set on trying to find them, at least stack the deck in your favor by utilizing a TPAM who knows these fund managers intimately. Then you can have active management between the funds you are using, as well as the funds themselves.

Other managers you might consider include, but are not limited to, Standard & Poor's and Loring Ward, or, on the ETF side, Vanguard. Your advisor may have other suggestions as well. This brings me back to how your FA fits into all of this.

You are probably thinking, if I am going to be using one of these TPAMs, what do I need an advisor for anyway? Well, there are a couple of reasons. One reason might be the value of having a professional help you evaluate your risk tolerance and the basic balance of your portfolio in the first place. Should you be 60 percent equity and 40 percent bonds or 40 percent equity and 60 percent bonds? Likely the TPAM is not going to make this initial decision for you. The advisor can also help you determine which TPAM is going to be best suited for your needs. Every one of the TPAMs I listed above has a very different management style and manager selection process, none of which are appropriate for every investor. You need to find a manager that you can trust, with a philosophy that you can get behind. Most importantly, though, you simply cannot access these managers directly unless you have $5M to $30M to invest. By utilizing a FA you can likely gain access to these managers with as little as $25K to $100K.

Another item you should discuss with your FA is your risk tolerance. Your FA should provide you with a risk tolerance questionnaire. This is a list of questions that helps guide them to an appropriate asset allocation to fit your needs.

You should also discuss your comfort level with certain asset classes like alternatives, (including mergers and acquisitions, long shorts, short only, private equity, commodities, futures, and market neutral), emerging markets, and high yield debt. All of these categories can add diversification to your portfolio. So, too, can they reduce the risk of your overall portfolio while potentially increasing returns, when used in moderation. However, when you look at any of these categories on a standalone basis, they can experience wide and sometimes violent swings. If you do not understand a particular asset category or are uncomfortable with it, I would recommend leaving it out of your portfolio to prevent unnecessary stress and potentially bad decisions. Personally, I do not touch anything involving shorts or market neutral. This is partially due to the fact that I do not understand what market neutral adds to the portfolio and largely due to the fact that short strategies only ever perform in down markets and typically involve active management.

Leverage is another topic that might come up in conversation. Feel free to discuss this topic in more detail with your advisor. I, for one, discourage any type of leverage. I will reserve an in-depth conversation of the topic for another time. Suffice it to say that leverage has been at the heart of every major bear market and is not a toy for the risk averse.

Lastly, you should have a thorough conversation about budgeting and income planning with your advisor. Be sure to review your current savings, income, income needs, and ongoing contributions to savings, as well as future income sources and income needs. Not every advisor will sit down with you to create a master budget plan for your family, but they should. And if they do not, you had better. You can find lots of different calculators online simply by Googling "budget plan" or going to www.dinkytown.com, one of my favorite sites for financial calculators. Then, of course, there is the budget we already created too.

Flying Solo

Whether you are going to go at it alone or not, I encourage you to read this chapter. It will provide you with a strong foundation in what your portfolio should look like, what to look for in investments, and potentially give you some ideas for questions you may want to ask your advisor. For those who believe they are ready to take their portfolio in their own hands, this section is a must read. In fact, read it twice just to be sure this is really what you want to do and you fully understand what is required to do the research and build your portfolio on your own.

I am going to break this section down into smaller parts focusing first on my personal favorites, ETFs, then on mutual funds, and, finally, wrapping it up with individual stocks.

ETFs and Basic Portfolio Construction

By far the easiest way, in my opinion, to go about composing your own portfolio is to utilize ETFs. I have already provided you with a solid list of asset classes that should be considered when constructing your portfolio. If you manage to choose a group of ETFs that can cover all of these asset classes, your job is nearly done. But we are getting ahead of ourselves.

As you start researching these ETFs, especially those in the more common asset classes, you might finds dozens of ETFs that cover the exact same segment of the market. So, how do you choose between them all? As you have already figured out, I am a huge proponent of low cost. Therefore, one thing to look at is the internal expense ratio of these ETFs. Typically, the lower the better. However, you are already looking at ETFs, so the internal expense ratios are likely very low to begin with. A more important point to evaluate is how well the ETF you are looking at tracks the market segment or asset class you are trying to capture. It does not bode well for your portfolio if your large cap growth ETF starts looking like your small cap value ETF, (however unlikely this may be).

Seeing as this is not the easiest point to evaluate, I will make it easy on you. Whenever possible, use one of the top ETF providers. There is something to be said about size, infrastructure, and ability to pass savings on-to your clients. iShares, SPDR, and Vanguard are the big three. You will also be pretty safe using PowerShares, iPath, or WisdomTree, though. Vanguard will almost always be your lowest cost, but iShares and SPDR may provide a better tool for tracking a particular market segment.

Some other items you will need to consider when constructing your portfolio with ETFs include how much you have to invest and the cost of trading. The more money you have, the more easily you can diversify into many ETFs. Similarly, the lower the cost of trading, the less impact these fees will have on your initial investment and ongoing rebalancing.

Ideally, you will need at least $10,000 to create a well-diversified portfolio without having trading costs eat you alive. $12,000 would be even better and anything over that will serve to reduce the cost of trading on a percentage basis. To give you something more concrete to work with, I would advise creating a portfolio of around 25 ETFs, preferably 30, and keeping your trading costs below 2.5% of your total investment. More on the trading cost later. For now, let us focus on the various levels of investable assets.

I would assume most of my readers are going to have accounts ranging from $50,000 to well over $500,000. If you fall into this category, you will find you can create a very well diversified portfolio using 25 to 30 ETFs. Even those with $1,000,000 or more may be surprised by the fact that they are probably not going to recognize additional benefits from diversifying above the 30 ETF mark. Later in the chapter, I will give you a couple of sample portfolios from which to use as a basis for constructing your own. The only reason you may want to add more ETFs to this structure would be to further narrow your focus on each market segment (small cap value, growth, and core, mid-cap, and large cap, financial, healthcare, international, etc), thereby creating additional flexibility to over and underweight each market segment, asset class, and region. Even by greatly narrowing your focus, you likely will not need more than 50 ETFs in your portfolio. As you can see, this first category covers a very wide swath of investors.

The next segment is for those just getting started. As I previously mentioned, you are really shooting for at least $10,000 to get your portfolio off to a good start. Acknowledging that we all have to start somewhere, it is far more feasible for many of us to drop in $50 or $100 per month. To be perfectly honest with you, you are going to have some growing pains with this method. First of all, many of the trading platforms you look at will require an initial deposit of $1,000.00, $3,000.00 or even $5,000.00. Furthermore, incurring the trading cost on a small investment of $50 to $100 dollars can have a detrimental impact on your earnings potential. What I would suggest is opening a checking, savings, or money market account in which you can make these monthly deposits. It will require a great deal of restraint on your part not to dig into these funds. With perseverance, though, you will eventually have enough money to make your initial deposit. After that initial deposit, I would still suggest building up sums of around $1,000 before making additional deposits into your investment account.

Keep in mind, too, that initial deposits will not be sufficient to fully diversify your portfolio with 25 ETFs. Instead, you will want to start with 2, 7, or 12 ETFs based on your initial investment being $1,000, $3,000, or $5,000, respectively. Once you reach the $10,000 mark you can fully diversify to 25 ETFs. At $12,000 you can expand to 30 ETFs if you desire. Everything above that is gravy. I say gravy because the more money you have to invest at this point, the less your trading cost will impact your investments, provided you do not continue to add more ETFs.

The important thing is that you get started as soon as possible. Even if it is as little as stashing $10 away per month. Everything helps and will pay huge dividends in the long term. All puns intended.

You will want to evaluate your own current situation, though. If you are carrying debt on your credit cards, have a home or car loan, or any other type of debt, you need to evaluate the value of paying this debt off early over investing your extra money. The first thing you need to do is figure out how much debt you have on each of your cards, loans, etc. and the interest rate you are paying on these debts. You will want to pay off the debt with the highest interest rate first! Now, whether or not you decide to pay off any of this debt prior to investing is another question entirely.

What you will have to figure out is how much you can expect to earn on any money you invest. If you are paying interest on any debt and the interest rate exceeds your expected rate of return on your investment, pay off the debt first. Otherwise, you may want to invest first. As a rule of thumb, if you are paying off debt, carrying an interest rate that exceeds six percent, pay off the debt first. Do not bother investing money until you have paid off this debt. Interest rates less than six percent are more questionable, but the closer the interest rate gets to zero, the more likely it is that you should go ahead and invest your extra money.

Having said all that, I highly recommend paying off all of your credit cards every month. You should never have to carry debt for anything other than large expenses like a house, car, or student loans.

Now, for the other end of the investment spectrum. For those with $5,000,000 or more, congratulations! Hopefully the rest of us will be there soon. When it comes to your portfolios you have several different questions to answer. First, I have already explained that you will not achieve additional benefits by expanding your holdings beyond 30-50 ETFs. So what can you do? Well, there are a couple of things you could look into. In all honesty, you may want to scrap the ETF selection process all together. Skip over the advisors while you are at it, too. Instead, call Russell, Vanguard, Avatar, or one of their ilk's directly, and find out what there minimum is to invest directly with them and have them build your portfolio for you in true institutional money management fashion.

Alternatively, use the portfolios I have constructed below as a starting point. From there, ask your friends what type of alternative funds and hedge funds they have been using. Look for funds that focus on mergers and acquisitions, managed futures, fixed income arbitrage, and private equity. Yes, these can be risky on a standalone basis. As part of the portfolio you are going to construct, though, they will provide diversification that actually reduces the overall risk of your portfolio.

The reason I bring these options up now is twofold. First, in order to invest in a hedge fund, you must be an accredited investor. For the individual investor this requires you either a) have a net worth that exceeds $1 million at the time of the purchase, excluding the value of your primary residence, or b) have an income exceeding $200,000 in each of the two most recent years or joint income with a spouse exceeding $300,000 for those years and a reasonable expectation of the same income level in the current year. Second, hedge funds are one of the least transparent vehicles available on the market. You will not always know what you are invested in. You will not always be able to access your money immediately. You will not always be able to access accurate performance information either. Hedge funds also tend to have much higher fees than most funds, due to their management styles. Both of these factors can be great deterrents for most people.   However, if you meet the first criteria and are comfortable with a lack of transparency, a few, well-chosen hedge funds can greatly enhance your portfolio.

One last item that investors with high net worth's should take into account is the tax consequences of their investments. Obviously the best approach is to avoid taxes altogether through the use of qualified accounts, (IRAs, ROTH IRAs, 401Ks, etc). For most high net worth individuals, this is not a feasible option. As you are probably well aware, there are limits on how much you can invest into these qualified accounts and certain income limits that prevent you from contributing to these types of accounts. You probably already have a number of non-qualified accounts set up as well. These non-qualified accounts are where we need to focus our attention.

At a very basic level, work on making your existing accounts more tax favorable. In order to accomplish this goal, you should use more tax favorable investments in your non-qualified accounts and tax heavy investments in your qualified accounts. It may come as a surprise to you but bonds are, as of the time of this writing, less tax favorable than stocks and other equity investments. The nice thing about stocks, mutual funds, and ETFs is they are only taxed at your income tax bracket if you have a short term gain or loss (less than 12 months). Provided you hold the security for more than 12 months, your gains, (losses), will be taxed at the long term capital gains rate of 15 percent. The same holds true for dividends. Bonds on the other hand are always taxed at your income tax bracket. Basically, if your income tax bracket is over 15 percent, you are better served to hold your bonds in a qualified account and your equity in a non-qualified account.

There are a few exceptions to this rule, though. Many alternative investments, limited partnerships, certain commodity investments, and things of that nature produce a, K-1. While the K-1 is not a huge burden, it will make your life a little easier during tax time if you can avoid having to report it. No one likes extra forms during tax season. By holding investments that produce K-1's in your qualified accounts you will not have to worry about filling this report come tax time.

These two suggestions are just to get you started. If you have been getting hammered by taxes due to gains in your non-qualified accounts, congratulations on making money in your investments when many individuals are not. Now, let's talk about how to help you keep even more of that money in your pocket. There are essentially two additional steps you can take to minimize your tax burden.

By far the most appropriate is to consult your tax advisor. Your tax advisor will help you evaluate what type of accounts to open that will potentially limit your tax burden now and in the future. Possibly the most valuable service your tax advisor can provide is guiding you on which accounts will best limit the tax liabilities encountered by your heirs when they inherit your estate.

A more immediate enhancement that can be made to your investments has to do with the style in which your investments are managed. Strategic, passive strategies tend to be more tax efficient than tactical, active strategies. So, too, are ETFs more tax efficient than most mutual funds. Taking tax management to the next level, you can also access certain managers, (like Russell or Lazard), who have portfolios that are specifically designed and managed to limit the tax burden those portfolios generate. In the past, you could also take tax management a step further utilizing a firm like Curian Capital. Curian has eight different tax lot preferences from which you can choose when you set up your account, including minimizing short term gains. Because Curian typically utilizes individual securities, they are able to continually manage your portfolio to meet your tax lot preference. Furthermore, you, your FA, or CPA, can access your account and do tax harvesting of your own, whereby, you select the securities that you want to sell in order to recognize those gains or losses.

Reuniting all of my readers I want to make you aware of another item you should be conscious of when evaluating the construction of your portfolio, (especially small accounts), as well as the platform you choose to use for constructing your portfolio. You are probably already aware of the multitude of platforms available to the retail investor for trading purposes. TD Ameritrade, E*TRADE, Scottrade, and Charles SCHWAB are just a few. The important thing is that you find a platform you are comfortable with and will provide the support and training you need to trade efficiently. One of the key factors you will need to evaluate is the trading cost for the platforms you are evaluating.

To give you a quick example, I use TD Ameritrade. With TD it costs me $4.99 per trade for stocks and most ETFs. I can trade 4 mutual funds per month for free. Outside of that, many ETFs and mutual funds fall under the no-transaction-fee category which means I do not pay a transaction fee for trading these funds ever. I believe new TD customers are charged $9.99 per trade for most securities, excluding those no-transaction-fee funds. Depending on the platform you decide on, your trading cost could range from $5 to $20, or even $50 per trade. If we look back at opening an account with 25 ETFs, that means our total trading cost could be anywhere from $125 to $500, or even $1,250, just to get started. That does not account for rebalancing. Clearly you can see why the trading costs of your platform are so important to evaluate. High trading costs can eat away at your invested principle and greatly impede your earnings potential.

There is one last item to evaluate before I get to the meat of portfolio construction. Now that you have decided which platform you want to use, you have to decide what type of account to open.

For those who already have accounts set up, feel free to skip this section and jump down to where I talk about building your ETF portfolio. For those just getting started, stay tuned and read on.

As usual, what type of account you open is going to depend on your individual circumstances. You can already begin to see why a financial advisor adds a great deal of value by helping with these types of questions. You should also consult your tax advisor when choosing the registration for your account, since they will be able to provide a far more in depth discussion on the tax benefits and consequences of each type of account, based on your circumstances.

Here are a few basic concepts to get you started.

Number one: should you open a retirement account, (qualified), or non-qualified account? If you are investing for retirement, are not going to touch the money until age 59 ½, and do not exceed the income limits to invest in a retirement account, by all means open a retirement account. If you fail to pass any one of these three requirements, a non-qualified account is more likely to be right for you.

Number two: if you are opening a retirement account, which retirement account should you contribute to? If your company offers a 401K, this is going to be one consideration. More to the point, if your company offers employer matching, (where they will match up to a certain percent of your contribution), the question is answered for you. Open and contribute to the 401K. Any time your employer will match your contribution, you can think of this as free money toward your retirement. If your company does not offer any type of match, forget the 401K. It is not going to have the options and flexibility that an individual retirement arrangement, (IRAs), will have. As for traditional IRAs vs. ROTH IRAs, it is going to depend on your current tax bracket vs. your future tax bracket and your earnings potential from interest.

Basically, do you think your current tax bracket is higher than your tax bracket is going to be at retirement or do you think your tax bracket will be higher at retirement than your current one? We cannot possibly guess how the tax brackets will change by the time you retire. What the financial industry typically assumes, though, is you will be earning less when you retire and will, therefore, be in a lower tax bracket at retirement. However, we also need to consider your earnings potential from the interest on your investments.

Essentially, the longer you have until retirement, the more interest you are likely to accrue, and the more you will potentially owe in taxes when you withdraw those funds. Therefore it typically makes sense for younger investors to go the route of the ROTH IRA, whereas older investors may wish to avoid taxes now, while they are in a higher tax bracket and pay them in retirement, hopefully, at a lower tax rate, with a traditional IRA.

Below is some useful information about the contribution and deduction limits on IRAs, as well as current tax brackets. This should help you determine which type of accounts you should, and can, contribute to.

2015 IRA Contribution and Deduction Limits - Effect of Modified AGI on Deductible Contributions if You are NOT Covered by a Retirement Plan at Work

If Your Filing Status Is...	And Your Modified AGI Is...	Then You Can Take...
single, head of household, or qualifying widow(er)	any amount	a full deduction up to the amount of your contribution limit.
married filing jointly or separately with a spouse who is not covered by a plan at work	any amount	a full deduction up to the amount of your contribution limit.
married filing jointly with a spouse who is covered by a plan at work	$183,000 or less	a full deduction up to the amount of your contribution limit.
	more than $183,000 but less than $193,000	a partial deduction.
	$193,000 or more	no deduction.
married filing separately with a spouse who is covered by a plan at work	less than $10,000	a partial deduction.
	$10,000 or more	no deduction.
If you file separately and did not live with your spouse at any time during the year, your IRA deduction is determined under the "Single" filing status.		

For up-to-date information on contribution limits, visit
http://www.irs.gov/Retirement-Plans/IRA-Deduction-Limits

2015 IRA Contribution and Deduction Limits - Effect of Modified AGI on Deductible Contributions If You ARE Covered by a Retirement Plan at Work

If Your Filing Status Is...	And Your Modified AGI Is...	Then You Can Take...
single or head of household	$61,000 or less	a full deduction up to the amount of your contribution limit.
	more than $61,000 but less than $71,000	a partial deduction.
	$71,000 or more	no deduction.
married filing jointly or qualifying widow(er)	$98,000 or less	a full deduction up to the amount of your contribution limit.
	more than $98,000 but less than $118,000	a partial deduction.
	$118,000 or more	no deduction.
married filing separately	less than $10,000	a partial deduction.
	$10,000 or more	no deduction.
If you file separately and did not live with your spouse at any time during the year, your IRA deduction is determined under the "Single" filing status.		

(IRS 2015)

For up-to-date information on contribution limits, visit
http://www.irs.gov/Retirement-Plans/IRA-Deduction-Limits

Table 1. 2015 Taxable Income Brackets and Rates

Rate	Single Filers	Married Joint Filers	Head of Household Filers
10%	$0 to $9,225	$0 to $18,450	$0 to $13,150
15%	$9,225 to $37,450	$18,450 to $74,900	$13,150 to $50,200
25%	$37,450 to $90,750	$74,900 to $151,200	$50,200 to $129,600
28%	$90,750 to $189,300	$151,200 to $230,450	$129,600 to $209,850
33%	$189,300 to $411,500	$230,450 to $411,500	$209,850 to $411,500
35%	$411,500 to $413,200	$411,500 to $464,850	$411,500 to $439,000
39.6%	$413,200+	$464,850+	$439,000+

(Pomerleau 2015)

You may also find sites like Dinkytown.com very useful in this decision making process. Dinkytown.com has a plethora of practical calculators. The following are just a few that will guide your current decision: Retirement Calculators (ROTH vs Traditional IRA), Tax Calculators (Marginal Tax Rate Calculator), and/or Finance Calculators (Home Budget Analysis)

Number three: for non-qualified accounts you need to first consider your status. Is an individual account appropriate or should you be looking at a joint account? Might a trust be more appropriate for your situation? These types of questions are best left to a tax professional.

Now that you have narrowed down your platform selection, as well as the account you are going to open, it's time to go about constructing your portfolio.

Historically, a well-diversified portfolio might have looked something like the following.

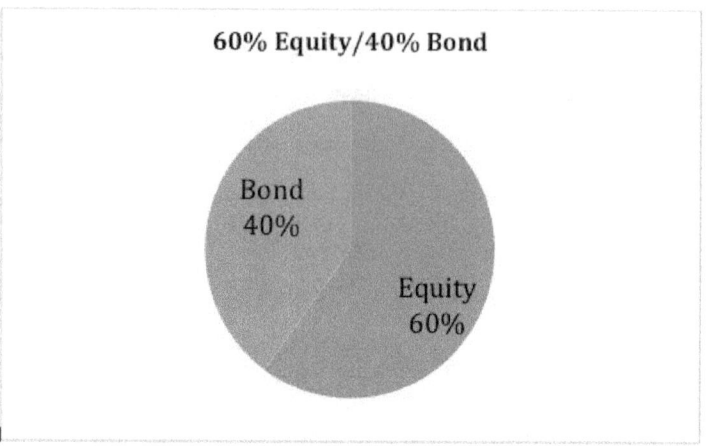

Inside of those broad asset categories you may have held a number of mutual funds. Thus your portfolio broke down to look more like this.

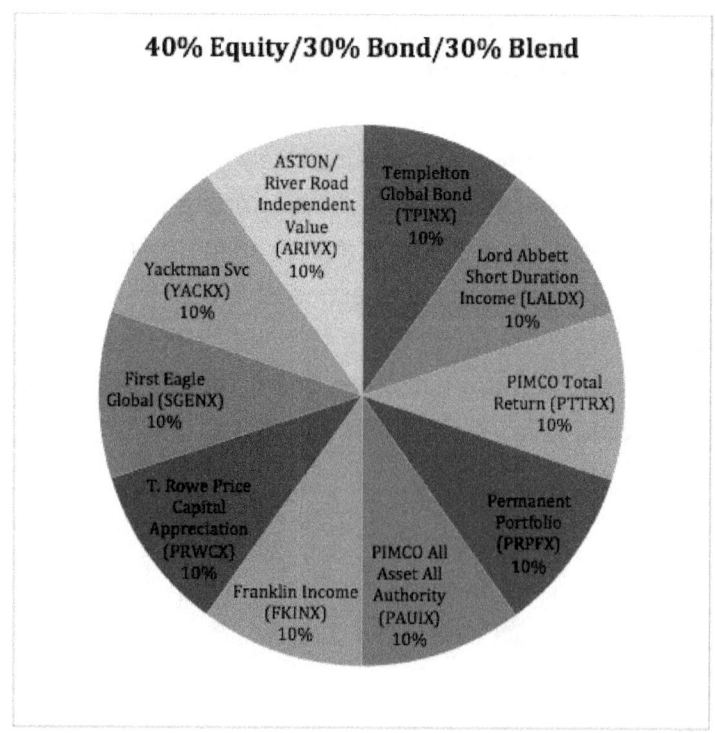

What you probably did not realize is how much control those mutual funds have over your internal investments. If you break down the above portfolio, which we would expect to be able to fluctuate from 40% equity/60% bonds to 70% equity/30% bonds, you would see that your portfolio looked more like the following.

39% Equity/49% Bond/12% Cash

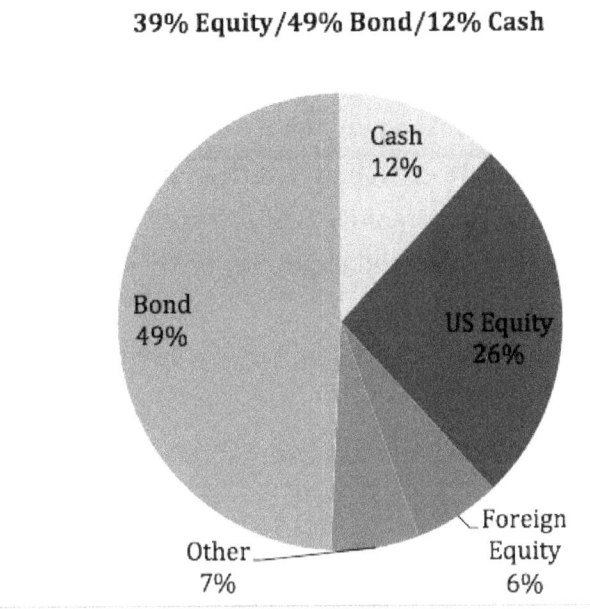

Some would argue that this, essentially, falls within the parameters above. I, for one, would not be happy paying the high cost of mutual fund management so that they could let 12 percent of my assets sit in cash. The reality of this cash position is even more startling. Many of these funds actually have close to 50 percent of their assets in cash. The only reason the portfolio nets out to 12 percent is that some of the other funds are short cash, (they have a net negative position to cash). You will also notice that only 6 percent of this portfolio is invested in international equity. Similarly, only 7 percent falls outside of the two broad asset categories of equity and bond. We hope that "other" encompasses some sort of alternative investments. Likely, we are looking at commodities and real estate, at best. Both of these provide some additional diversification to the portfolio, but not a sufficient amount to be meaningful.

Today, we know not only can we get better diversification than your basic 60/40 portfolio, but we need to have more diversification if we are to invest successfully over the long term. To give you an idea of where the smart money is going we will take a look at what the smart money is doing. Arguably, the smartest money in the markets are the large institutions like the Yale Endowment, which we will analyze here.

You may be surprised to find that the Yale endowment does not look anything like your traditional 60/40 portfolio. As a matter of fact, they would be hard pressed to get any further from the traditional 60/40 portfolio.

Below is a pie chart displaying the allocations for the Yale endowment in 2011.

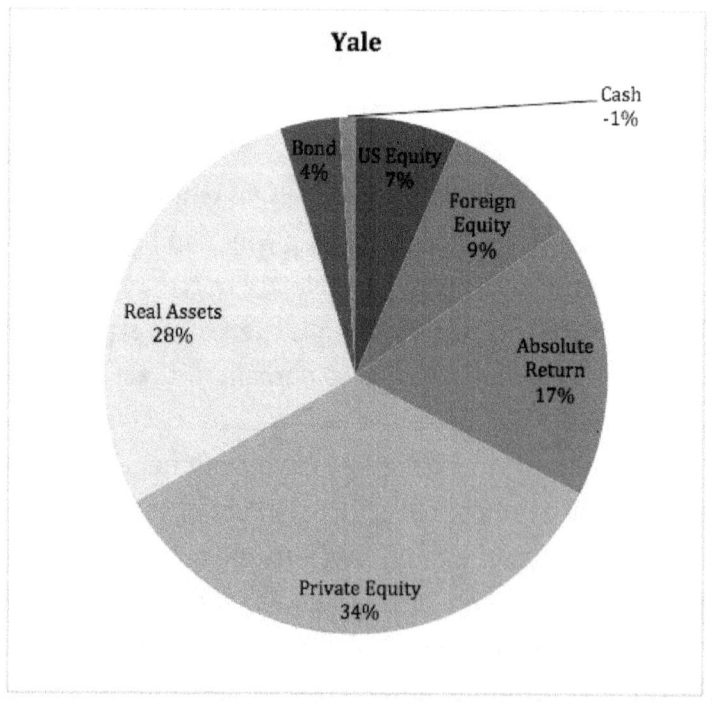

(Yale 2011)

Now that is a portfolio! Notice the complete lack of similarity between this portfolio, and the average investor's portfolio. Where most investors probably have 26 percent or more of their portfolio in US Equity, Yale has only 7 percent. Even more striking is the absence of bonds; 4 percent for Yale vs. 49 percent for most investors. You will also notice that Yale is not letting inflation erode their purchasing power by letting 12 percent of their investment sit in cash, but, rather, has a negative exposure to cash. The most important point of all is, the eye popping 79 percent exposure to alternatives as compared to the average investor's measly 7 percent. It is also important to note that the average investor's 7 percent likely consists of commodities and real estate. This is most similar to Yale's "real assets" of 28 percent. Therefore, the average investor is completely missing out on the opportunities presented by private equity and absolute return investments, which represent over half of Yale's portfolio.

All in all, Yale's endowment is roughly 97 percent equity or equity like investments, (equity like in terms of risk, as measured by standard deviation), and 4 percent bonds (with a negative 1 percent cash exposure). One could say this could easily be compared to an all equity portfolio. So, why did the Yale endowment perform so differently from the S&P 500?

Year	S&P 500	Yale
2007	5.49%	28.00%
2008	-37.00%	4.50%
2009	26.46%	-24.60%
2010	15.06%	8.90%
2011	2.11%	21.90%
Annualized Return	-0.25%	6.01%
Standard Deviation	23.99%	20.42%

(Yale)

The answer is simple, and not so simple, at the same time. The easy answer is: alternatives. But why did alternatives have such a dramatic impact on Yale's performance. Why was Yale able to annualize six percent, with three and a half percent less standard deviation, (risk), than the S&P 500, which annualized a negative quarter of a percent? Even though many alternative investments, like private equity and real assets can be just as risky, if not more risky, than most traditional equity investments, when used appropriately and combined in a well-diversified portfolio they can actually reduce the risk of the portfolio as a whole. You just have to close your eyes when it comes to intra year moves (short term fluctuations) within each individual piece of the portfolio.

The reason this works is due to the correlation, or lack thereof, of the various asset classes. For example, with a correlation coefficient of 0.05, private equity has almost no correlation to domestic e equity (http://www.nccr-finrisk.uzh.ch/media/pdf/wp/WP334_4.pdf). Similarly, real assets, like commodities and real estate, exhibit low to moderate correlations at 0.12 and 0.44, respectively. It is the independent movement of these asset classes that smooth out the investment rollercoaster. Thus, greatly improving the investment experience from the tangent and dependent movements of asset classes, like US large cap and small cap at 0.85. (Remember, a correlation coefficient of "1" is perfect correlation, "0" is no correlation, and "-1" is perfect inverse correlation).

If you think this might be a little extreme for your portfolio and your taste, you are probably right. Yale has much different liquidity needs than the average investor. And the one commonality between many alternative asset classes is their lack of liquidity. Yale also has a few more assets with which to play than the majority of us. This gives them the benefit of investing directly in these alternative asset classes, (especially private equity), whereas most investor's options are going to be severally limited. Because of the liquidity concerns and the limited investment options, I would advocate 10-30 percent of a portfolio be invested in alternatives.

We begin by first filling each asset category listed previously. At the same time, though, we want to be smart about how we fill each category.

For example, if we can use one ETF to cover large cap, value, blend, and growth, at one time, that might not be a bad thing to do. The obvious advantage is gaining broad market exposure without having to make multiple trades on multiple ETFs. The disadvantage is we lose our ability to overweight or underweight each of the three categories, (value, blend, and growth), relative to one another. Where you decide to consolidate and where you decide to fine tune is really up to you. I typically choose to consolidate whenever possible, with a few exceptions. Small cap value would be one of those exceptions. Certain commodities, like oil and gas or timber, would be another.

Below are five sample portfolios that you can use as guidepost when constructing your own portfolios.

Asset Class	Name	Ticker	90%/10% Percent	70%/30% Percent	50%/50% Percent	30%/70% Percent	10%/90% Percent
Domestic Equity	SPDR Dividend ETF	SDY	5%	6%	4%	3%	1%
	Vanguard Total Stock Market ETF	VTI	9%	6%	4%	2%	1%
	iShares S&P U.S. Preferred Stock Index	PFF	5%	6%	4%	3%	1%
	iShares Morningstar Small Value Index	JKL	7%	4%	2%	1%	0%
	iShares Micro-Cap ETF	IWC	6%	3%	2%	1%	0%
	Vanguard Utilities ETF	VPU	1%	1%	2%	1%	1%
International	Vanguard All-World ex-US ETF	VEU	7%	6%	5%	3%	1%
	Vanguard All-World ex-US Sm Cap	VSS	7%	5%	3%	1%	0%
	Vanguard Emerging Markets	VWO	6%	3%	2%	1%	0%
	SPDR S&P Int'l Dividend	DWX	5%	6%	5%	4%	2%
	iShares MSCI Frontier 100 ETF	FM	5%	3%	2%	1%	0%
Fixed Income	iShares Barclays Aggregate Bond	AGG	0%	2%	4%	7%	10%
	iShares Barclays 20+ Year Treas Bond	TLT	1%	4%	6%	7%	8%
	SPDR Barclays Investment Grade Floating Rate ETF	FLRN	1%	2%	4%	6%	8%
	iShares Barclays TIPS Bond	TIP	0%	2%	4%	6%	8%
	iShares IBOXX High Yield Corp Bond	HYG	2%	3%	4%	6%	8%
	iShares JPMorgan USD Emerg Markets Bond	EMB	1%	4%	6%	7%	8%
	SPDR Barclays International Corporate Bond ETF	IBND	2%	4%	7%	10%	13%
Alternative Assets	streetTracks Gold Shares	GLD	1%	1%	1%	1%	1%
	iShares Silver Trust	SLV	1%	1%	1%	1%	1%
	SPDR Wilshire Int'l Real Estate	RWX	3%	2%	2%	2%	2%
	Vanguard REIT	VNQ	4%	3%	3%	2%	2%
	SPDR S&P Global Natural Resources ETF	GNR	5%	6%	5%	4%	2%
	PowerShares Global Listed Private Equity Portfolio	PSP	7%	5%	3%	2%	1%
Alternative Strategies	Powershare DB G10 Currency Harvest Fund	DBV	1%	2%	2%	2%	2%
	ProShares Merger	MRGR	3%	3%	2%	3%	3%
	iPath S&P 500 Dynamic VIX	XVZ	1%	1%	1%	1%	1%
	WisdomTree Managed Futures Strategy	WDTI	2%	2%	2%	2%	3%
	Horizons S&P 500 Covered Calls ETF	HSPX	1%	2%	4%	5%	5%
	Calamos Market Neutral Income	CMNIX	1%	2%	4%	5%	7%

Note, that I never suggest going 100 percent equity or 100 percent bonds. As you can see in the graph below, a 100% bond portfolio is actually more risky than a 25% equity/75% bond portfolio. On top of that, you get better returns from the 20/80 portfolio. So why in the world would you go 100% bonds? While the distinction between a

100% stock portfolio and an 80% stock/20% bond portfolio is not as definite, you can see how you are not being rewarded as much for the additional risk you are taking. What I mean by this, is when you move from a 60% equity/40% bond to an 80/20 you increase your expected return by .7% and you increase your risk, (standard deviation), by 5%. Therefore, for every one percent increase in return, you increased your risk by 7.14%. However, when moving from an 80/20 portfolio to a 100% equity portfolio you increased your expected return by .6 and you increased your risk by 7%. Therefore, for every one percent increase in return, you increased your risk by 11.67%. This is not nearly as good a trade off as the first scenario. That is also why I do not think it is worth having a 100 percent equity portfolio.

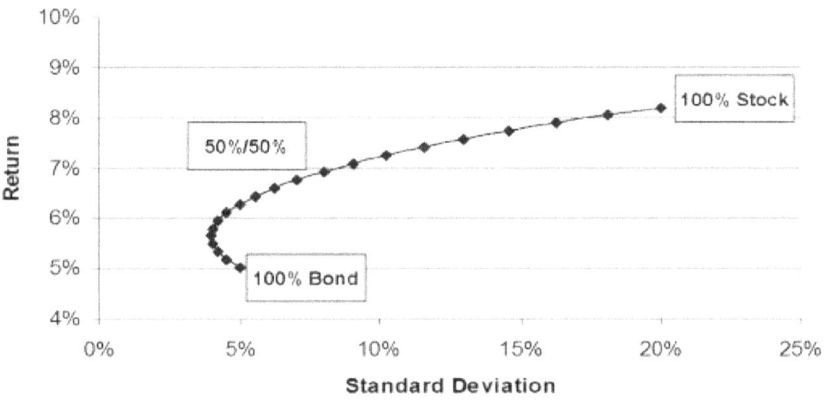

(Sigma Investing 2007) http://www.sigmainvesting.com/investing-basics/portfolio-theory-and-market-efficiency

A couple of additional notes before you go to town with your new shopping list. The above portfolios are samples only. They reflect my own personal preferences and are not necessarily appropriate for all investors. In fact, I would be remise if I told you I thought the 10% Equity/90% Bond portfolio was appropriate for anyone. While my own portfolio looks very similar to the 90% Equity/10% bond, these portfolios are to be used as guideposts only.

Items that you might consider altering within your own portfolios include, but are not limited to, the following biases I have built into these samples: 1) I like dividend paying stocks and preferred stocks both for growth and for income. Not everyone would agree with me on this point, especially given the relative underperformance of dividend paying stocks during the first half of 2012. 2) I tend to overweight small cap and value. This is a very long term view and a more aggressive stance than many investors are comfortable with. 3) I have a very small allocation to long term treasuries, not because I do not believe in them, but because I do not like the near term prospects for long term fixed income investments. I do not know how long it will take, but, eventually, my view on this asset class may take a complete 180. 4) You could feasibly scrap GLD and SLV in favor of GNR, since GNR technically incorporates all of these commodities. This would save you trades but would not necessarily get you exposure to these individual commodities in the same way. For example, GNR might hold shares of companies that mine gold, whereas GLD actually holds the bullion. 5) CMNIX is the only mutual fund included in the ETF portfolios, due to that fact that I have not uncovered a viable ETF to represent this strategy.

A few additional notes on alternatives to be aware of: One of the most common misconceptions about gold is that it is conservative and that it protects during down markets. Yes, gold tends to do well when the market is doing poorly. However, gold has, historically, been more volatile than the S&P 500. On top of that, up until recently, gold provided a lower rate of return than inflation, meaning you lost money relative to inflation by holding gold. For both of these reasons, I view gold as a diversifier and nothing more.

DBV, PSP, XVZ, WDTI and MRGR are the truest forms of alternatives in these portfolios, which is why I tend to overweight them. DBV is taking advantage of global macro trends via currencies.

PSP invests in private equity. XVZ is my best attempt at mimicking the VIX; a measure of volatility that cannot be directly invested in, but tends to go up during down markets. WDTI is a managed futures strategy investing in commodity, currency, and US treasury futures. MRGR employs a merger arbitrage strategy.

Now that you have a brief background on a few of these ETFs and your shopping list, you have some homework ahead of you. That is right, there is no free lunch. You do not get to simply take this list and build your portfolio. I told you before, the most dangerous thing you can do with your portfolio is invest blindly. Your job now, is to look up all of these ETFs. You can use Morningstar, Yahoo finance, Google finance, or MSN money, your trading platform, or whatever suits your fancy. However, you do your research you need to understand what each ETF is, what it invests in, what section of your portfolio it fits into and why. Until you have reached this understanding, do not invest a dime.

Mutual Funds

In this next section, I am going to do my best to provide some guidance on constructing your portfolio using mutual funds. As I have already mentioned, this is not my preferred method, so bear with me. The underlying rules for portfolio construction are going to be the same. Start by choosing a mutual fund that fits into each asset class I have previously listed. Since you will undoubtedly come across dozens, if not hundreds, of mutual funds that fit into each category, there are two things you can do to filter this list.

First, internal expenses are one of the most important things you can evaluate on a mutual fund. The higher the internal expense ratio, the better the mutual fund must perform just to show positive returns. Therefore, the lower the internal expense ratio, the better. Second, you need to look at the top holdings of your funds. When you look at these holdings you are looking for two things. One, make sure none of the funds you choose have the same top holdings. Each fund is designed to fit a specific piece of your portfolio and should look very different from the other funds. You want to avoid overlap as much as possible. Two, check to make sure these holdings fit within the category you are trying to match. You do not want your large cap growth fund holding small cap value or vice versa. That defeats the purpose of diversification.

Now, let's see if I can provide some additional guidance. Below are 5 sample portfolio's using mutual funds, similar to those I created for the ETFs. Keep in mind, these are only samples and are not necessarily appropriate for every investor, or any investor, for that matter.

Asset Class	Name	Ticker	90%/10% Percent	70%/30% Percent	50%/50% Percent	30%/70% Percent
Domestic Equity	Oppenheimer Rising Dividends N	ONRDX	5%	6%	6%	4%
	Schwab Market Track All Equity Investor	SWEGX	10%	8%	5%	3%
	Principal Preferred Securities A	PPSAX	5%	6%	6%	4%
	Putnam Small Cap Value A	PSLAX	13%	8%	3%	1%
International	Schwab International Core Equity	SINCX	5%	4%	4%	3%
	Putnam International Capital Opp A	PNVAX	7%	5%	2%	1%
	Amana Developing World	AMDWX	10%	7%	3%	1%
	SunAmerica International Div Strategy	SIEAX	5%	6%	6%	3%
Fixed Income	Laudus Mondrian Intl Fixed Income	LIFNX	1%	6%	10%	15%
	Madison Mosaic Government Y	MADTX	1%	5%	9%	15%
	Putnam American Government Income	PAGVX	1%	4%	8%	12%
	Wasatch-Hoisington US Treasury	WHOSX	0%	2%	4%	3%
	Schwab Treasury Inflation Protected Secs	SWRSX	1%	5%	9%	13%
	Pax World High Yield Bond Individual Inv	PAXHX	3%	4%	5%	6%
	Invesco Emerging Mkt Lcl Ccy Debt Instl	IIEMX	3%	4%	5%	6%
Currency/Alts	Eaton Vance Parametric Struct	EAPSX	4%	2%	2%	1%
Alternatives	Natixis ASG Diversifying Strategies	DSFAX	6%	4%	3%	2%
	Calamos Convertible Arbitrage	CVSIX	3%	2%	1%	1%
	Natixis ASG Managed Futures	AMFAX	3%	1%	1%	1%
	Franklin Gold and Precious Metals	FKRCX	2%	2%	2%	1%
	Putnam Global Natural Resources	EBERX	3%	2%	0%	0%
	Van Eck Global Hard Assets	GHAAX	1%	1%	1%	0%
	Goldman Sachs Commodity Strategy	GSCAX	1%	1%	1%	2%
Real Estate/Alts	Schwab Global Real Estate	SWASX	3%	2%	2%	1%
	Davis Real Estate Fund	RPFRX	4%	3%	2%	1%

Individual Securities

Our last portfolio construction method revolves around individual security selection. In this section, I am going to provide you with the most important things I look for when choosing to invest in an individual company, rather than using a mutual fund or ETF. This method is not designed to be an all-inclusive portfolio construction method, but rather a method for taking over a small segment of your portfolio. Just as I do not expect a financial advisor, or even a mutual fund manager, to be an expert on every segment of the market, I freely admit that I am not either.

Because I am not an expert at everything, I have chosen to fine tune my expertise. In my case, I feel far more comfortable doing my own security selection on the large cap, domestic, equity portion of my portfolio. You can see how narrow this field really is. I am not trying to manage the domestic bond portion of my portfolio, the small cap, or any of the international investments, for that matter. The fact of the matter is, the only portions of my portfolio I am taking full control of, provided I was using my ETF portfolios, are SDY and VTI. The rest of my portfolio will remain unchanged.

You may have your own area of expertise, in which case, you may want to take control of a very different portion of your portfolio. My goal is simply to show you how to go about it and share with you my limited knowledge of security selection in an area I have chosen to focus.

When creating my stock portfolio, I want to build a safe portfolio that I can be confident in for the long term. I am looking to hold these companies for an average of ten years or more and I want to be reasonably sure they are not going out of business in that time. Hence, the reason I narrow my search to large cap, quality stocks. The S&P 500 is an easy way to meet the first criteria. To further ensure I meet the first criteria, I also only look at companies with market capitalization greater than $5 billion. (This limited my search to 412 companies). The rest of my filters will help ensure we meet the quality filter too.

Ultimately, we are looking to narrow down on 25 to 30 companies, so we have a ways to go from our original 500. While it is not exactly a value play, my next step is to throw out any stocks with prices below $5 per share or over $50 per share. (This narrowed my search to 210 companies). I am not looking to risk my money on penny stocks or seriously out of favor companies. Nor am I looking to pay too much for a company. I am not saying there are not many companies out there that are worth more than $50 per share, just that the simple math does not promote investing in these companies. Think of it this way: If you buy a stock for $5 per share and it goes to $10 per share, you made 100% on your money. If you buy a stock for $50 per share and it goes to $55 per share, you have the same $5 per share gain, but you have only made 10 percent on your money. That is a big difference.

Furthermore, my own research, using multiple regression analysis, indicates that the purchasing price of a stock is one of the best indicators of future performance when that security is held for a minimum of 10 years. It sounds too simple to believe, I know. The math supports it though. As does the old maxim, "buy low and sell high."

This also coincides nicely with the value philosophies of some of the most successful investors in history. Buffett, Graham, and Templeton were all value investors. So, too, were they long term investors. Buffett held his stocks for a minimum of ten years. Price held his stocks an average of five years. (Ross 2000)

The next filter I use is the dividend yield. Like many of the investors I mentioned a moment ago, I am a big dividend investor. If a company is not paying a dividend I do not even bother. My ideal company has a dividend yield between 2 and 10 percent. (This further narrowed my search to 122 companies). This is not much of a limiting factor. I am just trying to weed out the outliers. Especially those companies paying more than 10 percent, as this is often a sign of future troubles, however counterintuitive that may sound. I would also like to see companies with a track record of paying out those dividends for the last three years, at a minimum. Over that period, I want to see a steady growth in those dividends, too. I do not want sporadic dividend payouts and I do not want excessive growth in dividends. Sporadic dividend payouts are a sign of uncertainty and excessive dividend growth or high payout are unsustainable.

You can already see how much a dividend can tell you about a company. This alone should be enough to take note. Wait until you see what it does for your investment. Imagine you invest in a company paying just a 2% dividend for $10 per share. That is only $.20 per share annually. Let's say over the next 10 years the share price grows from $10 per share to $20 per share. Your annual return, just from appreciation, is 7.18%. Now, let's factor in that dividend assuming it maintained at $.20 per share. Your $10 investment is now worth $22 and your annual return jumps to 8.20%. Had you reinvested those dividends your investment would have been worth $22.79, making your annual return 8.59%. That is a difference of 1.41% annually. Not too shabby, considering we are not even accounting for dividend growth.

Before we move on, let's take a look at a less positive scenario. Assume we ran across another 10 year period that looked like the lost decade. Had our investment dropped to $9.5 per share, we would have lost .51% annually. Look familiar? Now, if we account for our dividend, instead of losing .51% annually, you would still have made 1.37% annually and your investment would be worth $11.46. That is a far cry from $22.79 and 8.59%, but it beats the heck out of -.51%. Hopefully, you can see the true power of dividends now.

The next item of interest is not so much a filter, as a way to sort your now narrow list of remaining securities. The cash flow ratio, (cash flow from operations/current liabilities), is one of many liquidity ratios. Specifically, I like the cash flow ratio for its dependents on cash flow from operations. Earnings are nice, (but can be manipulated), and current assets are good, but cash is king. If a company is not generating cash from their day to day operations, they are in for a rough patch. Sure, a company can use their financing capabilities to fund operations, as they should to a certain extent. But a true sign of strength is a self-sustaining company. Therefore, the higher the cash flow ratio, the better.

The biggest drawback to the cash flow ratio is having to gather the data. That is also the reason I had you narrow your list down as much as possible, prior to calculating this ratio. Once you have gathered that data on your remaining stocks, it is simply a matter of sorting those stocks by the cash flow ratio. Those companies with the highest cash flow ratio should be on top. You can probably see that sorting your stock list strictly on the cash flow ratio places a high dependences on this ratio. Depending so heavily on the cash flow ratio is not my preference, which is why I have developed the following methodology.

Readers, prepare yourselves to get deep into the weeds. The next few paragraphs and graphs will really only appeal and apply to a select few readers. If you have already started to bock at the amount of work that went into the first three criteria, feel free to skip this section, read to the end of the book, and re-read the section on ETFs or mutual funds. Otherwise, you have been warned.

It is time to get very intimate with Excel. Consider this your third and final warning of the chapter. The easiest way to go about sorting your list, (mine consists of 122 stocks), is to export everything to Excel.

First, to ensure adequate diversification, we want to keep as many different market sectors as possible. My list includes 11 sectors including basic materials, capital goods, consumer cyclical, consumer/non-cyclical, energy, financial, healthcare, services, technology, transportation, and utilities. Given that I would like to narrow down to 25 to 30 companies, my goal is to keep 2 or 3,

(30/11=2.73), companies from each sector. Of course, I also want the companies with the best investment prospects, too. However, two of my sectors have only one company, so they are in by default. For capital goods, Rockwell Collins, Inc., (COL), and for transportation, CSX Corporation, (CSX), are both in.

Keep in mind, I will have more sectors with three companies than I otherwise would have, to make up for the individual companies in capital goods and transportation. To be precise, I am shooting for 3 companies in each sector, (30-2=28, 28/9=3.11 [30, 2, and 28 are the number of stocks, and 9 is the number of sectors remaining]). Therefore, I have yet another default. Consumer cyclical has only three companies, so, all three, Ford Motor Company, (F), Johnson Controls, Inc., (JCI), and Mattel, Inc., (MAT) are all in.

Second, I need to sort the remaining sectors, to narrow down on my top 3 picks. I am still going to look at my three filters when I sort each sector. That means I am still sorting by price, dividend growth, (not dividend yield this time), and cash flow ratio. Below is my sort for Basic Materials. I have also performed this same sort for the remaining 7 sectors.

Symbol	Name	Price	Dividend Growth
CLF	Cliffs Natural Resources Inc	$ 41.57	1
DOW	The Dow Chemical Company	$ 29.65	3
FCX	Freeport-McMoRan Copper & Gold Inc.	$ 34.76	3
IP	International Paper Company	$ 34.34	3
NEM	Newmont Mining Corp	$ 46.63	1
NUE	Nucor Corporation	$ 39.56	3
PCL	Plum Creek Timber Co. Inc.	$ 40.20	2
WY	Weyerhaeuser Company	$ 23.86	3

Now that I have all of my data, I need to rank each company according to each criteria and assign a weighting for those criteria. In my case, I still view price as my most important criteria, dividend growth is second, and cash flow ratio is third. An easy way to weight these criteria is in reverse order of importance. Therefore, price is assigned 2, dividend growth 1.5, and cash flow ratio 1. You will soon see how this puts the greatest weight on price. Keep in mind, too, you can always change these weights or even your criteria based on what you think is the most important factor for predicting future performance. I am just showing you how I did it so that you can perform a similar filtering process on your own portfolio.

The ranking is easier. The company with the lowest price is 1, second lowest is 2, so on and so forth. Cash flow ratio is just the opposite. The company with the highest cash flow ratio is 1, the second highest is 2, and so on. Due to the fact that dividend growth is somewhat arbitrary, we will have to create our own ranking system. In this case, those companies who have not paid dividends every year of the last three years received a 4, those that paid out dividends but the amounts varied greatly received a 3, those that paid out a flat dividend the entire time received a 2, and those that had a steadily increasing dividend received a 1.

Since the dividend growth is one of the more complicated rankings, let me provide you with a few examples from basic materials. I previously mentioned three years, at a minimum. I happen to have easy access to five years' worth of data which is even better so, I will go with that.

Symbol	Name	2007	2008	2009	2010	2011	Standard Deviation	Rank
CLF	Cliffs Natural Resources Inc	$ 0.25	$ 0.35	$ 0.26	$ 0.51	$ 0.84	24.57%	1
DOW	The Dow Chemical Company	$ 1.64	$ 1.68	$ 0.60	$ 0.60	$ 0.90	54.01%	3
FCX	Freeport-McMoRan Copper & Gold Inc.	$ 0.69	$ 0.69	$ 0.08	$ 1.13	$ 1.50	53.38%	3
IP	International Paper Company	$ 1.00	$ 1.00	$ 0.33	$ 0.40	$ 0.98	34.51%	3
NEM	Newmont Mining Corp	$ 0.40	$ 0.40	$ 0.40	$ 0.50	$ 1.00	26.08%	1
NUE	Nucor Corporation	$ 2.44	$ 1.91	$ 1.41	$ 1.44	$ 1.45	44.76%	3
PCL	Plum Creek Timber Co. Inc.	$ 1.68	$ 1.68	$ 1.68	$ 1.68	$ 1.68	0.00%	2
WY	Weyerhaeuser Company	$ 0.94	$ 0.94	$ 0.24	$ 0.08	$ 0.60	39.47%	3

You will notice that none of these companies display a perfect steady growth in their dividends but that several of them come close, (CLF and NEW). In fact, with the exception of PCL, it's very difficult to eyeball this sequence of dividends and determine where they should fall. One method of aiding your decision process is to calculate the standard deviation of each set of numbers. In this scenario, I would plug the following equation into Excel: "=stdev(C2:G2)", for CLF. From there, I can drag this equation down by clicking and dragging the lower right hand corner of the cell down through the other rows. I have chosen 33.33% as my cutoff for a company receiving a 1 vs a 3. You can argue that this is somewhat arbitrary and you would be right. Very little in finance is an exact science.

A couple additional items of note from the above chart: You might be tempted to say that PCL should receive a 1 because it has the lowest standard deviation, or because it has never lowered its dividend. The drawback to PCL's steady dividend is it is not growing and will, therefore, not help you keep pace with inflation. You may also come across a company with a very low standard deviation where the dividend has been decreasing every year. This company should not receive a 1 either. You are most certainly looking at another 3, no matter how low the standard deviation is. You will also notice that we do not have any 4s in our sampling because every company has paid a dividend for at least 3 years, and in this case, 5 years.

Below is my ranking chart for basic materials.

Symbol	Name	Price	Dividend Growth	Cash Flow Ratio
CLF	Cliffs Natural Resources Inc	7	1	1
DOW	The Dow Chemical Company	2	3	7
FCX	Freeport-McMoRan Copper & Gold Inc.	4	3	3
IP	International Paper Company	3	3	8
NEM	Newmont Mining Corp	8	1	2
NUE	Nucor Corporation	5	3	5
PCL	Plum Creek Timber Co. Inc.	6	2	4
WY	Weyerhaeuser Company	1	3	6

Once we have our ranking, we can apply our weighting. All this requires is multiplying the ranking by the assigned weighting. Therefore, all of the numbers in the price column will be multiplied by 2, (the heaviest weighting), and dividend growth will be multiplied by 1.5. Once these columns are multiplied by their weighting, we can total the score for each company. All of these calculations can be seen below.

Symbol	Name	Price	Dividend Growth	Cash Flow Ratio	Total	Rank
CLF	Cliffs Natural Resources Inc	14	1.5	1	16.5	4
DOW	The Dow Chemical Company	4	4.5	7	15.5	2
FCX	Freeport-McMoRan Copper & Gold Inc.	8	4.5	3	15.5	2
IP	International Paper Company	6	4.5	8	18.5	5
NEM	Newmont Mining Corp	16	1.5	2	19.5	7
NUE	Nucor Corporation	10	4.5	5	19.5	7
PCL	Plum Creek Timber Co. Inc.	12	3	4	19	6
WY	Weyerhaeuser Company	2	4.5	6	12.5	1

The company with the lowest overall score wins. Rather, the companies with the three lowest scores win. In the case of a tie, go with the company you feel more comfortable sticking with for the long term. WY, DOW, and FCX will all find a place in my portfolio.

Having completed the same analysis for the remaining sectors, I came up with the following list for my final portfolio. All of these are to be equally weighted, again for diversification purposes.

Sector	Company 1	Company 2	Company 3
Basic Material	DOW	FCX	WY
Capital Goods	COL		
Consumer Cyclical	F	JCI	MAT
Consumer/ Non-Cyclical	CAG	HRL	SPLS
Energy	MRO	VLO	WMB
Financial	CINF	HBAN	SLM
Healthcare	BMY	MDT	PFE
Services	KIM	RSG	WU
Technology	AMAT	GLW	INTC
Transportation	CSX		
Utilities	CMS	PEG	XEL

There are several additional things you will want to keep in mind if you choose to select individual securities for your portfolio, aside from the obvious work involved. One) every one of these stocks will involve an additional trade that can really add up when compared to the two ETFs they are taking the place of. Two) you no longer have a manager to rebalance this portion of your portfolio, so you will have to rebalance these stocks every 6 to 18 months. Three) you now have to monitor these companies to make sure they are not in danger of going out of business. Four) you will have to re-run your screen every 10 years or so, to update your list and replace companies that you had to remove.

Good Luck!

Whether you have chosen to construct your portfolio using ETFs, mutual funds, individual stocks, or some mixture of these options, you have to continue to monitor your portfolio. I am not talking about watching it daily, weekly, or even monthly. Emotions run far too high in the short term to avoid irrational trading decisions. I am talking about rebalancing and keeping abreast of the changing financial environment.

You have built your portfolio with the intent of providing solid diversification, given your specific tolerance for risk. If you allow your portfolio to run, unattended, for too long, certain holdings are bound to outperform others. This will cause your portfolio to shift its risk tolerance, (likely become more risky than you want it to be), and, potentially, lose the advantages of diversification you worked so hard to build into it. That is why you have to rebalance your portfolio.

Personally, I rebalance my portfolio semiannually, (every 6 months). Technically speaking, this is not in my own best interest. Research tells us that the optimal rebalancing schedule is every year and a half, (18 months). I will leave it to you to determine the optimal frequency to rebalance. Whatever you decide, I would recommend staying between 6 months and 18 months. Less than 6 months tends to be too frequent, leading to overtrading and overanalyzing, and more than 18 months will lead to forgetfulness and neglect.

You also need to keep yourself abreast of continued enhancements in investment vehicles and what is considered an alternative. Keep in mind; it was not that long ago that mutual funds were a novel idea. Diversification at that time meant holding a handful of stocks and maybe some bonds. A mutual fund provided complete diversification all in one place. Now people hold a multitude of mutual funds. Even that does not seem to be enough today.

The whole idea was to increase your diversification to reduce your risk without sacrificing returns. That is why people started mixing stocks and bonds in their portfolios. As the correlation between the traditional 60/40 portfolio and the S&P 500, (100% equity), grew closer and closer to 1, (perfect correlation), the idea of alternatives sprung up. Alternatives were investments that had a low correlation to the market. REITs, (real estate investment trusts), currencies, and commodities were the first attempt at accessing alternatives. Today, we have access to an even wider array of alternatives that offer even lower correlations to equity markets. I have already discussed these alternatives in detail in previous chapters. The point is, the concept of diversification is ever changing. People have said that modern portfolio theory, (MPT), is dead. The truth is, MPT is not dead, it has just evolved. So keep up and keep yourself abreast. These portfolios are not the end all, be all. They too, will eventually be out of date and new alternatives, or some idea no one has ever even heard of, will be the wave of the future.

As one final reminder, do not be influenced by the news, media, hype or hysteria. If you take nothing else away from this book and do nothing else with your portfolio, turn off the news, toss out the financial section of your newspaper, and stop listening to your friends, family, and Cramer. Give your portfolio a break and let it do what it was designed to do. It was not designed to provide 12%

annual returns year in and year out, without fail. It was designed to provide positive 20's, negative 15's, more extremes, and everything in between. You cannot recognize a smooth average return until you have held your portfolio for at least 10 years, and preferably 20.

Once you have built your portfolio in a manner that suites your risk tolerance, financial needs, and retirement goals, let it ride. Rebalance occasionally, take new ideas with a grain of salt, do your research on additional means of diversification, and understand what you are invested in and why. Aside from that, take the one good piece of advice Cramer offers at the beginning of every show, **"Stop Trading"**!

References

CBOE, www.cboe.com/micro/vix/historical.aspx, 2012

Dalbar, Inc. www.dalbar.com, 2012 QAIB

IRS, "IRA Deduction Limits", http://www.irs.gov/Retirement-Plans/IRA-Deduction-Limits, 01/20/2015

iShares, http://us.ishares.com, BlackRock, 2012

Johnson, Roger N., "Bad News Revisited: The Portrayal of Violence, Conflict, and Suffering on Television News", Peace and Conflict: Journal of Peace Psychology, 2(3), 201-216, Lawrence Erlbaum Associates, Inc. 1996

Lang, Annie, Park, Byungho, Sanders-Jackson, Ashley N., Wilson, Brian D., and Wang, Zheng, "Cognition and Emotion in TV Message Processing: How Valence, Arousing Content, Structural Complexity, and Information Density Affect the Availability of Cognitive Resources", Media Psychology, 10:317-338, Lawrence Erlbaum Associates, Inc., 2007

Loring Ward, "Performance Summary" disclosure, www.loringward.com, LWI Financial Inc., 2012

Pomerieau, Kyle, "2015 Tax Brackets",
http://taxfoundation.org/article/2015-tax-brackets, Tax Foundation,
08/02/2014

Ross, Nikki CFP, "Lessons from the Legends of Wall Street : How
Warren Buffett, Benjamin Graham, Phil Fisher, T. Rowe Price, and
John Templeton Can Help You Grow Rich", Kaplan Business, June 19,
2000

Random.org, www.random.org, Mads Haahr, 2012

Singh, Ramadhar, Kaur, Susheel, Junid, Fazlinda B., and Self, William
T., "Reacting to headline news: Cicrumstances leading to causal
explanations versus implicational concerns", International Journal of
Psychology, 2011, 46 (1), 63-70, 2010

State Street Global Markets,
http://statestreetglobalmarkets.com/research/investorconfidenceind
ex/, 2012

Szabo, Atilla and Hopkinson, Katey L., "Negative Psychological Effects
of Watching the News in the Television: Relaxation or Another
Intervention May Be Needed to Buffer Them!", International Journal
of Behavioral Medicine, 2007, Vol. 14, No. 2, 57-62, Lawrence
Erlbaum Assoehciates, Inv., 2007

UBS Wealth Management Americas, www.ubs.com, 2012